A Wild Rough Lot

A Wild Rough Lot

Whaling and Sealing
from the
Moray Firth

Malcolm Archibald

Copyright (C) 2012 Malcolm Archibald
Layout design and Copyright (C) 2019 by Next Chapter
Published 2019 by Reality Plus – A Next Chapter Imprint
Cover art by Evit Art
All rights reserved. No part of this book may be reproduced or transmitted in any form or by any means, electronic or mechanical, including photocopying, recording, or by any information storage and retrieval system, without the author's permission.

Acknowledgements

I would like to thank the following people for their help while I was compiling this book:
   Mr Graham Wilson, Archivist, Moray Heritage Centre, Elgin
   Mrs Chris Reid, Fraserburgh Heritage Centre
   Mr Jim B Campbell, Canada
   The staff of Fraserburgh Museum
   Mr Iain Flett of Dundee City Archives
   Mrs Rhona Rodger, Curator, McManus Museum, Dundee
   Robbie and Dot Stephen, Fraserburgh

For Cathy

Introduction

Whaling and sealing are evocative subjects today. Extensive media coverage of the actions of environmental groups have brought the world's attention to the plight of seals and the great whales in a way that would have been incomprehensible when Moray Firth ports sent ships to the hunting grounds. The attitudes and actions of the nineteenth century were vastly different from those of the twenty-first; hunting was a popular sport and whales were seen as a valuable commodity rather than a fellow species deserving of conservation.

To the Greenlandmen, the mariners who sailed the ships and hunted the whale in the waters of the Greenland Sea and the Davis Strait, whaling was a job. It may have been tinged with romance and spiced with adventure, but essentially it provided a wage that paid the rent and clothed and fed the family. At its peak in the 1850s nine whaling and sealing vessels sailed from Moray Firth ports. That was a significant percentage of the Scottish total, and the Arctic adventure certainly contributed to the local economy.

The mid nineteenth century was an exciting time to be alive, with the destitution years of the Hungry Forties past and innovation, enterprise and confidence blossoming. The coast of the Moray Firth was no exception, with new ventures being considered, and sealing was suddenly on the agenda as a commercial possibility. The Victorians had a zest for life and the Moray Firth ports entered the Arctic trade as if it was a great adventure, commercialism tinged with the sheer joy of trying something new. Whatever one's feelings for the rights or wrongs of hunting seals and whales, there can be no denying the raw courage the seamen needed to venture into the iced waters of the north in a small sail powered vessel, never knowing what tomorrow would bring, never knowing if they would return home to their wives and children.

Three ports of the Moray Firth sent ships north: Fraserburgh, Banff and Nairn, while Inverness toyed with the idea and Garmouth and Lossiemouth had tentative connections. Of the three, Fraserburgh was the most successful, with Banff next and Nairn not really getting anywhere.

This small book will show something of the sealing and whaling industries of the Moray Firth coast. It will start with a brief look at the Moray coast, and then give an overview of the industry. There is a chapter giving what could be a typical voyage, followed by a chapter on sealing, the Nairn and Banff experience, a brief look at the dangers the whaling men faced and two chapters on Fraserburgh's time as a sealing and whaling port. Finally there are lists of ships from Banff and Fraserburgh.

When this book was first compiled, it was intended to give endnotes for every detail, but the end result was a text littered with numbers that made reading a chore. It was decided to write a free-flowing book instead; easier to read and with the main sources mentioned within the text. The book gives anecdotes, names and a few details. It is not intended to justify an industry that is today in public disfavour, nor is it in any degree an exhaustive study, but it should sketch the outline of a time when Fraserburgh and Banff send hardy men to the hunting grounds of the Arctic circle.

Chapter One

A MARITIME BREED OF MEN

Again for Greenland we are bound
To leave you all behind
With timbers firm and hearts so warm
We sail before the wind
The Whaler's Song – traditional

Burghead was never a whaling port but it is an enigma. It is a small fishing village on the south coast of the Moray Firth, about 37 miles east of Inverness and 69 miles west of Fraserburgh. Any visitor will immediately surmise that here is something special, although they might not immediately know why. It is not a large place, but built on a north thrusting promontory that ends in a curious, grass covered mound with an old signal station on top, and affording splendid views of huge stretches of the Moray Firth.

There are many places along this coast that give good views, but Burghead is different somehow. There is an atmosphere here, an aura of great age and of something else, watchfulness nearly, that alerts those who have the perception that they are somewhere unique. There are other places with this atmosphere; DunAdd in Argyll is one, and

Edinburgh Castle, another. They were all ancient fortifications, Dark Age settlements where Stevenson's "silent races" now slumber in all but memory.

The mound at the tip of Burghead's promontory is all that remains of what was once a prominent Pictish fort, and the relentless grid-iron pattern of Burghead's streets were planted upon the remainder, thus destroying what might have been one of the most valuable archaeological sites in Northern Europe.

There is no mistaking the strategic location of Burghead fort. On a promontory, surrounded by sea on three sides and with an easily defendable neck of land on the fourth, it is a natural stronghold for a maritime people. And that is the point. Only a people secure in their mastery of the sea would choose such a site, for it is as near an island as a shore based fort can be, and if besieged, could be easily supplied by sea. There is no doubt that the Picts, or Cruithin, were a sea going people, and the coastline of the Moray Firth was their home.

The Moray Firth is that huge mouth of northern Scotland that roars eastward toward Europe. It is the largest and most northerly indentation on the East Coast, marked at either extremity by dramatic promontories and fringed with some of the most picturesque and historic communities in the country.

Kinnaird Head, at the knuckle end of the Buchan fist, marks the southern end of the firth, and in its shadow sits Fraserburgh, that most maritime of Scottish towns where a still thriving fishing fleet provides employment and a focus for the community. From here the coast stretches westward, passing cliffs where the sea fumes, glorious and amazingly empty beaches and a host of small towns and tiny villages. The names are evocative with history: Rosehearty and Crovie, Macduff and Banff, Portsoy and Buckie; Lossiemouth, Burghead and Nairn. In some, fishing boats still provide employment, but others are attempting to re-invent themselves with tourism or heritage. Marinas of pleasure craft now take the place of harbours filled with brown-sailed Zulus or Scaffies, and tourists photograph dolphins where fishermen once cast hopeful nets.

The southern coast of the Moray Firth ends at the hinge of Inverness, then alters direction to slice north eastward, past the smaller Dornoch Firth and Loch Fleet to Clearance haunted Sutherland and the great gaunt coastline of Caithness and some of the most dramatic cliffs of Europe. At last, in the very north eastern extremity of mainland Scotland, Duncansby Head places a final full stop to the firth. It is a fittingly emphatic ending to a coast of unending drama, a place of wild sea and unconquerable land. To look south from here is to view a peerless geographic panorama, but even the keenest observer could not see into the past.

The Picts of Burghead were only one of the maritime peoples who made this beautiful coastline their home. Between the retreat of the great ice caps and the beginning of recorded history, the Mesolithic hunter-gatherers paddled through the marshes to merge, a few millennia later, with the Neolithic people. If, as is often assumed, the Neolithic people arrived by canoe, skirting the coast from the south, then they were the first seamen in the Moray Firth.

The Bronze Age arrived much later, followed by the Celts with their superior iron tools. More centuries past and Roman galleys carried the imperial eagles to the north, but their visit was fleeting; they came, saw but failed to conquer. Nevertheless, their visits did help to put the Moray Firth coastline on the map. It may have been the example or the threat of Rome that encouraged the local tribes to merge into larger groups, but from around the third century after Christ the Picts were the dominant people here. Presumably the Picts were a combination of all the indigenous peoples under a warrior aristocracy that may have been the last Iron-age immigrants. For long a people shrouded by ignorance, current research is unearthing many facts about these Picts, so they are gradually emerging from the haze of history as less than mysterious. There was a Pictish monastery at Portmahomack within shouting distance of the Firth, and where hand-working monks made books. Around this coast, carved stones reveal that the Picts eased from pagan superstition to Christianity at about the same time as other peoples in what is now Scotland.

Picts would clash with invading Scots along this coast, and then came the Norse. Either Scots or Norse ravaged Pictish Burghead, but while the Scots remained, the Norse withdrew westward and northward, beyond Inverness. From their capital at Dingwall, the Norse remained a threat, making this a Scottish frontier every bit as volatile as that with England hundreds of miles to the south. The kingdom of Scotland had to balance two borders in order to survive, so it is no wonder that the Province of Moray boasts so many monuments to the past.

As the Scottish kingdom pushed its border north, hard-won peace came to this coast and the maritime peoples put down their swords and searched instead for other pursuits. By the end of the 11th century the Moray Firth was bounded on three sides by a united Scotland and on the fourth by the North Sea. Trade was a natural continuation of peace, and the people of the Firth exchanged goods with their overseas neighbours. Trading towns such as Inverness, Banff and Fraserburgh sent ships to Europe and south to other ports of Scotland. Fishing became a major industry, with Wick and Balintore, Fraserburgh and Lossiemouth, Buckie and Brora all sending their quota of boats into the often-stormy waters of the Firth. There was also boat building, with nearly every fishing community larger than a village making and repairing the local craft, and larger scale enterprises at Garmouth, Lossiemouth and Buckie. The sea was vital to the people of the Firth, and the northern waters bred hardy seamen. It is hardly surprising that when sealing and whaling offered lucrative opportunities, many local seamen donned their foul weather gear and looked to the north.

Chapter Two

THE SCOTTISH WHALING INDUSTRY

*'With Riff Koll Hill and Disco dipping
There you will see the whale fish skipping'*
Traditional whaling saying

To see a whale at sea is to witness one of the wonders of the world. There is nothing quite so awe inspiring as to be in a boat when the great fin emerges from the water, and to witness the flukes of its tail wave a final goodbye is heart wrenchingly beautiful. These are magnificent oxygen breathing mammals that survive underwater and roam the seas by right. Yet from time immemorial humanity has hunted them, both by driving them ashore singly or in great pods, or by taking boats to sea to kill them in their own environment.

By the middle of the 19th century humans were so expert in hunting that they had driven the whales to the furthest, coldest oceans of the north so that every whale hunt was a perilous adventure for man as for animal.

The Scottish whale hunters were principally after the Greenland Right Whale, *Balaena Mysticetus,* as it was slow in the water and floated once killed. A good specimen might weigh around one hundred tons and stretch for over sixty feet, which was two thirds the length of the early whaling ships and over twice as long as the whaleboats from which they were hunted. They are distinctive creatures, designed to swim and with a layer of blubber that serves to maintain their body heat even in conditions of extreme cold, although it is believed that the species originated in warmer waters, where most return to breed.

Until well into the nineteenth century, whales were regarded as very large fish, and the whaling industry was known as whale fishing. The Greenland Right whales were distinctively smooth backed and swim slowly at perhaps five knots, which suited the wind powered sailing ships and their oar-powered boats. Greenland Right Whales also floated when killed, which was a great bonus to men in an open boat with maybe ten miles to row back to the mother ship. The Scottish Arctic whalers were not after the sperm whales, but they did kill narwhals when they could and actively hunted polar bears and just about anything else that could make them a profit or provide some sport.

Why?

Why should humans ever hunt these truly magnificent animals, whose grace and power have the ability to inspire awe and even love? Why should man venture into some of the most dangerous environments anywhere, to stand in a tiny boat and thrust a piece of iron into a monster some eighty or a hundred feet long, knowing that if there was every chance the boat could capsize or be lost amidst the ice? Why did man risk his limbs and life through frostbite, accident or disease to kill something that had never done him any harm, and which he quite possible admired?

The answer is simply for necessity and profit. People need to live, and money made life possible. Many whaling masters and many of the crewmen sailed north year after year, becoming expert in what was a highly specialised field. For instance the Stephen family were involved in the industry from its first year in Fraserburgh until it ended in that port, and then migrated to Peterhead, where they continued as seamen, if not Greenlandmen, as the whaling and sealing sailors were known. While one Stephen commanded the Fraserburgh whaling ship *Melinka*, his brother was master of the Fraserburgh sealer, *Vulcan*. Other men joined the crew for a season or two, either to make money for some other endeavour, or from a sense of adventure. But life in the Arctic was not for everybody. While many continued in the business for years, others found that a single trip was enough. However, all had one thing in common; they were professionals, hunting for money to feed their families, and the company owners invested their money in the industry, hoping for a profitable return.

When the industrial revolution increased in crescendo in the late eighteenth and early nineteenth century, it created a growing demand for whale oil and whalebone. A decent sized Arctic whale could carry nine tons of oil in the form of blubber, which was taken back to Scotland to be boiled in special boiling yards. The resulting oil was used for soap and paint, as well as for lighting that made the shockingly dangerous Georgian and early Victorian streets safer. John Dyson in his book *The Hot Arctic* mentioned that whale oil was used in London's first street lamps, and thus contributed greatly to the safety of that city. While those who walked the city streets might bless the new fuel, it is doubtful if factory workers agreed, for now their masters could keep them toiling for much longer hours in often horrendous conditions.

When gas emerged as an agent for lighting and heating in the early decades of the nineteenth century, the demand for whale oil dipped, but it was also useful in the woollen industry and later, when mixed with water, for softening raw jute. The jute industry of Dundee helped keep Scottish Arctic whaling alive until well into the twentieth century.

The whale hunters also brought home baleen. The Greenland Right Whale swam on the surface, catching krill in its open mouth. The food was filtered through overlapping plates of baleen and the unwanted seawater ejected. This baleen - or whalebone - could sell for as much as £3000 a ton, so that the catch of even a single decent sized whale could make a voyage profitable. Whalebone had a multitude of uses, but for a long period it was vital in the women's fashion industry. In the eighteenth century, fashion dictated that ladies should have slim waists, which in many cases argued for the use of corsets. Being flexible but tough, whalebone was an excellent material with which to make corsets, so the demands of female fashion contributed to the death of thousands of Arctic whales. Whalebone, however, was a versatile material and was also used for brushes, umbrella canes, whips and stuffing, frames for fashionable hats, fishing rods and nets, gratings and just about anything that required a material that was both flexible and strong.

Whaling then, was important for the lifestyle of 19th century Britain. As with every industry, it continued as long as there was a demand for the products, but would fade once cheaper alternatives were available, or when culture and attitudes altered. Throughout the nineteenth century, few people would consider killing a whale as wrong. When the ports of the Moray Firth entered the trade in the 1850s, such an idea would have been inconceivable.

Scottish commercial whaling had a chequered beginning. At the beginning of the seventeenth century the Dutch were the European masters of whaling, but King James VI and I attempted to challenge this hegemony by creating whaling companies in Scotland and England. When the Leith based Scottish East India and Greenland Company received a thirty-five year patent in 1617, it sent a single ship north. Although it was moderately successful, opposition from the English Muscovy Company caused the Scots to withdraw. Eight years later a second attempt by a Leith company had the same result and Scottish whaling slithered into non-existence for decades. Further Scottish attempts in 1670 and 1682 were equally unsuccessful and the century closed on a low of economic stagnation, failed colonies and one of the worst famines ever to hit Scotland. The so-called Ill Years were a fitting end to what had been a turbulent century.

The opening of the Eighteenth century did not promise much better as in 1707, racked by dynastic and religious troubles, Scotland entered into a political union with the one nation that had been her enduring enemy. The result was Great Britain. The new entity was born out of necessity rather than desire: Scotland needed trade and religious security, while England needed to know her northern border was safe during her constant European wars. With the nightmare of a French-Scottish alliance haunting the dreams of English statesmen, it is little wonder that many in South Britain rejoiced when Scotland was enticed, bribed or threatened into a union that was contrary to the wishes of the majority of the Scots.

For decades the Union did little for Scottish trade and nothing for the whaling industry. The Dutch continued to dominate European whaling, selling their oil and baleen to Scots and English markets while the Scots merely watched. It was King George who decided to again challenge the Dutch supremacy. As well as economic reasons, he had an ulterior motive, for if Great Britain possessed a successful whaling fleet, it would also have a reservoir of hardy seamen who could be pressed into the navy in time of war.

The difficulty about starting the whaling industry was in persuading merchant adventurers to advance their wealth in such a hazardous occupation, but bribery, in the form of a bounty system, eased away that block. Accordingly, in 1733 the government proclaimed they would pay a bounty of £1 for every ton weight of a ship over 200 tons that ventured on the whaling trade. There were strict stipulations, however: every vessel had to carry forty whale fishing lines of 120 fathoms, forty harpoons, six months' provisions, four boats for the actual hunting, five first voyagers or 'Green Men'; and, most unusually, a surgeon.

To ensure that they actually sailed north and did not merely pocket the bounty and remain in port, there were strict regulations for these whaling companies. Each ship had to be measured by the Customs Officer. Each owner, master and mate had to take an oath that they were bound for the whale-fishing grounds. Each ship had to keep a log to record their voyage. If the government was to help finance this industry, it wanted it properly regulated and controlled.

British merchants, however, were too wary to be so easily bought, and few bit at the silver harpoon. By 1749 Britain floated only two whaling vessels. Not until 1750, when the government doubled the bounty did investors seriously consider the whaling trade. A bounty of two pounds sterling for every ton weight over two hundred tons may not sound a lot, but in 1750 such a sum could cover the expenses of a whaling voyage. The merchant adventurers were limiting their liability, and if successful, would still reap the profit. Companies sprang up the length of Britain, from London in the south to Aberdeen in the north. At that early stage, there were no takers from the Moray Firth. The canny merchants of the north preferred to hold their wealth, watch the voyages of the whalers and wait for results.

Although it was obvious that the government took nothing on trust, the whaling companies flourished. Leith became a whaling port, with Aberdeen following and the first of the Dundee vessels sailing north by 1754. There were also ships from Dunbar and Montrose, Burntisland, Kirkcaldy and Bo'ness, but the Moray Firth ports remained quiescent. They had no need to venture quite so far north as they traded with their long-standing partners in Europe. The risks of whaling were not worth the margin of profit.

While the Scottish whaling industry made mainly tentative steps to the Arctic, the English took giant strides, with London and Hull floating fleets of whalers. However, despite government help, the British Arctic whaling industry remained smaller than other nations. The Dutch continued to be a formidable force, while the vessels of the North American colonies thrust forward to dominate the supply of whale related products to Great Britain. Only after the American Revolution and the birth of the United States did the British whaling industry really explode. As they were no longer part of the Empire, the whaling men of the ex-American colonies lost their trade advantages; some immigrated to Britain and brought their expertise with them.

. Although English ports were still the more important in Britain, Scottish ports were proving their mettle. Dunbar and Leith, Bo'ness and Kirkcaldy, Dundee and Montrose all sent ships north. Then, in 1788 Peterhead, just around the corner from the Moray Firth, first looked to the whaling and sealing trade. The first Peterhead vessel was *Robert*, of 169 tons and was English commanded and largely English manned. Captain Peacock took her north each season for the following decade, but with only moderate success. On two of these ten years she came home 'clean' or empty of whales, and her best ever catch was a mere three whales. By the end of that decade it became apparent that there was something wrong with the good ship *Robert*, and there was speculation that Captain Peacock and many of his English crew had accepted annual bribes from English whaling companies to fail. It was believed, perhaps correctly, that the southern ports wanted to maintain their stranglehold of the whaling trade.

Accordingly, in 1798 Mr J Arbuthnott and Mr John Hutchison of Peterhead pressed for a change of personnel. Captain Peacock and his English followers were dismissed and Peterhead men hired in their place. With the local Captain Gearey in command, *Robert* was more successful in her eleventh season, catching four whales, which produced 71 tuns of oil. However, that was only the beginning, with double the number of whales caught the following year, producing 96 tuns of oil. Peterhead had finally begun to show the success that was to turn the town into Britain's premier whaling port.

In 1802 the Peterhead whaling company replaced *Robert* with the larger *Hope*, of 240 tons, and that season Captain Gearey caught eleven whales. The expansionist trend continued in 1804 when Peterhead doubled its fleet by adding the 290 tons *Endeavour*. Yet Peterhead was still only a tiny cog in the British whaling industry, with London, Hull and Whitby far more important, and other East Coast Scottish towns sending ships in ones and twos. It was not until 1810 that Peterhead purchased *Active*, but at 308 tons she was a fine large vessel. *Perseverance* of 240 tons came the following season, and a decade of good fishing, as the whaling was known, saw further increases in the fleet, despite the danger of United States attack during the American war of 1812 to 1814.

The total of Peterhead ships rose steadily: six in 1813, eight in 1815, eleven by 1818, which revealed that whaling was not only successful, but prosperous at a period when much of Britain was experiencing an ugly recession and there was social and political turmoil in the country. In 1820 Peterhead increased its fleet to eighteen ships and the Greenlandmen raised the roofs of the taverns of the town.

As if to show that the sea must never be taken for granted, the upward trend halted and levelled into a plateau. No new ships were added to the Peterhead whaling fleet until 1825 and the sea began to take its toll. Northern whaling was always a dangerous trade, with the constant danger of storms augmenting the hazards of ice, snow and the lash of a whale's tail, but so far Peterhead had been fortunate. In 1822 she lost *Invincible*, and next year the 321-ton *Dexterity*. Not surprisingly, interest in the whaling trade slumped and in 1827 only thirteen ships sailed north from Peterhead.

There were three more ships lost in 1828, when the veterans *Enterprise* and *Active*, were among those that failed to return. Again confidence was shaken, but twelve ships headed for the Arctic in 1829, and all returned safely. 1830 proved one of the worst ever years for the British whaling industry, with two Peterhead ships among the nineteen lost that year. The large, 400-ton *Resolution* was one, and *Hope*, Peterhead's second ever whaler, was the second. Twenty-one further British ships returned to their homeports clean of whales. That year marked the beginning of a bad decade, with Peterhead sharing in the general malaise. In 1831 the port lost *James*, but after that the number of whaling vessels remained static. Eleven vessels sailed out, and eleven returned, but if there were no further losses, neither was there spectacular success.

In 1836 the Peterhead vessels brought back a meagre total of six whales and 86.5 tuns of oil. As the crew's wages was based on a small monthly figure augmented by a share of the profit of the whale oil, a low catch meant disappointed wives, hungry children and men desperately seeking employment. Not surprisingly, only ten whaling ships sailed north the following two years. As it seemed that whaling was fading, the masters, ship owners and shareholders hoped for a further source of revenue to justify their investment in the whaling fleets, and they found it in seal hunting, or seal fishing as it was known at the time.

In 1837 some British vessels tried seal hunting and made a profit. The following year it was apparent that sealing was more profitable and less dangerous than whaling, so in 1839 the bulk of the Peterhead fleet augmented their whaling activities with sealing. Twelve ships sailed north, a number reduced to eleven in 1840 when the old *Perseverance* was lost.

However, despite the surge of hope, some ships were still unsuccessful, and losses continued to reduce Peterhead's fleet. From eleven in 1841, there were ten in 1842, and only five whales were caught. However sealing provided a bloody lifeline for the Arctic seamen, with 15,000 seals killed by Peterhead vessels that same year. 1843 was slightly better, so the number of ships in this roller-coaster trade increased by one the next year. A new working pattern emerged, with some ships sailing to the sealing in the Greenland Sea seal fishing and then returning home, while others sailed on to the Davis Strait whaling.

. Sealing proved lucrative, and the number of Peterhead vessels fluctuated according to the success of the port, so in 1851 fifteen Peterhead vessels killed 83,000 seals and in 1852 there were twenty-two vessels. The success of Peterhead sealing attracted the attention of speculators and merchants along the Moray Firth coast and in 1852 other ports entered the northern sealing trade. The next few years were to be very interesting.

The local population showed great interest in the trade. They mustered in their hundreds to watch the ships depart. In 1859 Gordon Stables, an Aberchirder born student doctor who later became a Royal Navy surgeon and an author of boys adventure stories, wrote: "the whole of the bonnie wee town was down to see us start, and really there were more tears shed than there were handkerchiefs to dry or wipe away." He sailed north in the brig *Vulcan* that year.

Both the sealing and whaling trade demanded a considerable capital outlay, particularly after the bounty system ended in 1824. There were three major drains on any whaling company's capital: the ship, the provisions and the wages for the crew. Of these, the ship came first for it took a special kind of vessel to survive in the Arctic ice.

Arctic whaling vessels had to be incredibly strongly built to withstand the terrible conditions in which they would work. The hulls were 'doubled' which meant they had an extra layer of planking, with either a third layer on the bows, or sometimes a covering of iron. The ice could damage even these iron plates as Surgeon Trotter of the Fraserburgh vessel *Enterprise* pointed out on the 16th June 1856: "several of our defensive iron plates are gone."

Some vessels may also have been strengthened by ice beams, which were beams of wood about 12 inches (30 centimetres) thick as internal bracings. In the early period, and well into the 19th century, the whaling vessels were known as 'blubber boats' and were short, about 100 feet long, stubby and immensely strong. The smell on a whaling ship when full of blubber was said to have been shocking, so perhaps there was a good reason for other vessels treating them with scorn.

At first the vessels carried great casks into which the blubber from the whales was placed, but after the middle of the 19th century many were fitted with iron tanks, which made the storing of blubber easier. The whalers carried more men than ordinary trading vessels, as the crew had to both sail the ship and row out in small boats to hunt, kill and bring back whales. The largest of the ships might carry as many as seventy men, with the smallest still having thirty-five. At the beginning of the twentieth century, small ketches with crews of around a dozen were heading north, but they represented the dying kick of the Scottish Arctic whaling industry.

Rather than being paid a flat rate, the Greenlandmen received a fixed wage plus a bonus that depended on the amount of oil they brought home. On a good voyage this oil money could account for the bulk of their wages, and helped encourage the hands to hunt the whales, which was probably the most dangerous part of their job.

There are many examples of the often-violent behaviour of the Greenlandmen, who were as tough as any seamen afloat. The Moray Firth seamen seemed no different from the general run of whaling men, and Surgeon Trotter on the Fraserburgh vessel *Enterprise* in 1856, mentioned their general demeanour, in particular the swearing: "the terrible oaths and curses I got used to."

The whaling vessels themselves did not partake in the hunting but acted as mother ships, sending out small boats which held five, six or seven men and which did the actual harpooning and killing. It was easy for these small boats to get lost among large icebergs, or in a fog, or to get blown away by a sudden storm. Alexander Trotter's journal has many mentions of fog such as "still very thick, clearing up occasionally for a few hours and then coming down as bad as ever...when one gets up in the morning and asks, 'is it thick yet?" the answer invariably seems to be "...as thick as buttermilk or brose." And again "it came down thick so that we could not see near half way to her, i.e. the boat, so we fired guns off every now and then, and blew through a trumpet to let them know whereabouts we were." The mention of the trumpet is interesting, as there is an example of such a foghorn in the fishery museum in Anstruther, used by Captain Smith of Cellardyke in Fife. It is remarkably small for the purpose, made of metal and to a generation used to technological aids for everything, seems grossly inadequate for the purpose.

It was also easy for whaling ships; particularly sail powered vessels, to be stuck in the ice. Again Trotter mentions this fact: "a great many ships have got beset in the ice, unable to get out again at present." The ice also gripped *Vulcan* when Stables was on her in 1858. She was icebound for six weeks of seal hunting and worry, with the occasional scare as bergs nipped the ship. All the time she drifted south of Jan Meyer. Captain Stephen ordered a channel carved through the ice, and the hands struggled with ice saws and gunpowder to get *Vulcan* free. She escaped, to find she was only in a long water channel of water within the pack ice and had to bore through, with the hands rowing the boats and fending off the ice as the music of the fiddle gave them cheer.

That facet of whale hunting was quite common, with many journals and accounts of the high latitudes having at least one mention of vessels trapped in the ice. John Nicol, one of the few eighteenth century before-the-mast mariners who left a written account of his life, also mentioned it: "we were for ten days completely fast in the ice… and the ship was so pressed by it everyone thought we must either be crushed to pieces or forced out upon the top of the ice, there ever to remain."

In 1834 the Dundee vessel *Dorothy* was stuck and the master, Thomas Davidson "called all hands and warped the ship through." Even as late as 1884, when most whaling vessels were steam powered, the ice could be formidable, as this short passage by Matthew Campbell, who sailed in the Dundee vessel *Nova Zembla* shows: "at 12 pm stuck fast in the ice and backed astern but of no avail. Called all hands to roll the ship, which they did with a will, so much in fact that her boats almost touched the ice."

The possibility of storms was also present. Trotter spoke of heavy weather: "clear today but with a tremendous sea: forced to take two of our boats on deck [from hanging over the side] and also to block up one of the stern windows."

Sometimes there was no wind at all, and rather than having a holiday, seamen engaged in whale hunting had to work harder than ever. For example in the Dundee whaler *Dorothy* in 1834, when there was a period with hardly any wind the master "called all hands to tow the ship." As with the towing of *Vulcan*, the boat's crews sang while they rowed.

A whaler's life was certainly not for milk-and-water seamen but suited only the hardest working and most stanch of seamen. Luckily, the Scottish ports produced a plethora of such men. Most of their actions would go unrecorded, but one recorded seaman was James Sim from Broadsea by Fraserburgh. He is only known because he married Christian Watt, a Broadsea woman who included him in her amazing journal. At over six feet, James Sim was tall, and certainly brave, for he had helped save the crew of a Norwegian ship in trouble off the west coast and patriotic, having volunteered for the Navy during the Crimean War. Today he may have become a celebrity, but in the middle of the nineteenth century he was merely another Scottish seaman, risking his life every time he put to sea and living on poverty wages.

Given that wages were similar along the coast, although it seems that the men picked up in Shetland were paid less, the rates for Peterhead, published in 1858, would probably be typical for whaling and sealing seamen for the Moray Firth ports during the same period. The mate was paid £4 15/- (£4- 75p) per month, with a bonus of 6/- (30p) per tun of oil money and 2/6 (12.5p) for every 1000 seals. The second mate was paid £3 per month and 6/- per tun of oil and 2/6 for every 1000 seals. A specktioneer, the head harpooner who was responsible for the harpoons and other whaling equipment, was paid £3 per month, with 6/- per tun of oil and 1/6d per tun of whale bone (baleen), 2/6d for every 100 seals and a sum that varied from 16/6 to (82.5p) to 31/6 (£1 – 57p) for every whale he harpooned.

The other harpooners were paid £3 per month, 6/- per tun of oil, 2/6 per 100 seals, the same amount of harpooning a whale. Boat steerers, who guided the whaleboats when hunting the whale, were paid £3 a month and 3/- per tun of oil money. Able seamen were paid £2 10/- (£2-50p) per month and 1/6d (7.5p) per tun of oil money, with ordinary seamen paid from £2 to £2 5/- (£2- 25p) a month and 1/3d (6.5p) to 1/6d per tun of oil money. Lastly there were the Green Hands, those first voyagers who had never been to sea before or, later, who had never sailed in a whaling ship before, who were paid between 35/- (£1-75) and £2 per month with 1/- (5p) per tun of oil money.

Although this table did not include the master, Innes MacLeod in his *To the Greenland Fishing* claimed he would be paid a figure of £7 or £8 a month. While these wages seem ridiculously low today, they were better than most seamen earned, so long as the vessel was successful. It can be easily seen that the more whales the ships caught, the better the wages of the whaling men, and how those at the bottom end of the pay scale would want to rise beyond the rank of Green man to become at least an ordinary seaman and probably aspired to become a harpooner. To an extent, the system was fair as the greater the responsibility in a whaling vessel, the higher the rewards.

The ship's owners, however, knew that these relatively high wages added to the expenses of the voyage. Financing a whaling ship was no light burden, for while the rewards could be great if a ship caught a number of whales, the Arctic was a dangerous place and many ships were sunk or damaged. Even if the ship returned unharmed, unless it caught a fair quantity of whales and seals, the owners would be out of pocket as they still had to pay the crews keep and wages. The owners would be desperate for a successful shipmaster, a man with just the correct blend of daring, caution and luck to take the ship into dangerous waters and bring her back safely with a full cargo.

Such a master was a prized man, but he had to possess many talents. Basil Lubbock, in his *Arctic Whalers*, included an excellent chapter on the qualities needed by a whaling master. Lubbock said that the captain had to be a natural leader who gave confidence to his men. He had to understand the Arctic weather, ice and stars. He had to be able to take his ship into unchartered waters and passages with the right combination of caution and daring. He had to make instant and correct decisions, using excellent seamanship and having intimate knowledge of the job of every man on board. A lucky captain was the best of all, and when Captain Stephen left the Fraserburgh vessel *Melinka* in 1868 some murmured that her good fortune departed with him. If a whaling master was lucky, the crew would follow him. Captain Markham, a Royal Naval officer who sailed as an unofficial passenger on the Dundee whaler *Arctic* in 1873, mentioned that the master, Captain Adams, always carried a lucky penny with him.

Naturally, not everybody agreed that whaling masters needed a variety of skills. By law, whaling ships were required to carry a surgeon, and these were mainly young men in their early twenties, either students looking for money or recent graduates looking for experience. Many of these men left a journal recording their experiences, and being young, their writings are full of strong and not always favourable opinions. In 1834 John Wanless sailed on the Dundee vessel *Thomas* and said that 'the abilities of Masters of whaling fishing vessels are highly praised and valued when they prove successful but...let it suffice that the qualifications of a whaling captain are very limited."

A typical Greenland voyage would cost around £1,500 per sail powered ship, which was a lot to invest with no guarantee of return, and more for the coal fuelled steam ships. For that reason whaling and sealing companies were generally composed of a number of individuals so the risk was spread more thinly. Many of these owners would know little about the sea. They would, however, be aware that the longer the voyage and the deeper the ships penetrated into the icy seas of the north, the more dangerous and more expensive it would be.

In the majority of cases, a company was formed for a single ship, or a number of ships, and people, men or women, bought a single share or a number of shares in the vessel. The minimum investment, one share, was one sixty-fourth part of the ship, and investors would often have shares in a number of vessels in case a particular ship was sunk or damaged. There were occasions when ownership of any individual vessel changed hands in a bewildering fashion. The Dundee whaler *Friendship* was a case in point. Originally a prize of war captured from the French, *Friendship* was registered in Dundee in 1827, owned by the Friendship Whaling Company, with owners that included the merchants David Ouchterlony and Robert Stirling and the bookseller George Miller. In December 1828 these three transferred their shares to Thomas Nicoll, a Dundee merchant, who sold four sales to Thomas Davidson, ship master on the 10th of February 1829. Ten years later Mrs Charlotte Robertson or Nicoll was one owner, along with Mrs Margaret Nicoll or Ross, possibly her sister- in-law and Mary and Ann Nicoll with James Brydon Nicoll and Charlotte Nicoll. Three years after that Mrs Margaret Davidson, widow of the shipowner Thomas Davidson was the sole owner.

Ship owners, then, were not always loyal to their vessel, which was often only a method of making money. Many did not have a strong maritime connection; the first Dundee screw steamer, *Tay*, was partly owned by George Alison and William Strong, wine merchants, who also had shares in *Dundee*, while the Fife farmer, Peter Christie owned three shares in *Camperdown*. The Dundee vessel *Horn* also had a variety of owners with no obvious maritime knowledge or interest. As well as the merchants James Gray and Robert Stirling, there was at one time or other, George Miller the bookseller, John Mackay the hatter and Andrew Powrie the tobacconist. In the case of *Eliza Swan*, the Montrose whaling ship however, the sole owner was Eliza Swan, wife of a Mr John Brown.

The Moray Firth vessels would have a similar broad base of ownership, but unfortunately the company documents have not survived.

It will be noted that not all the shareholders were men, but women did not just have shares in whaling ships. They could also become involved in the business. Christian Watt, wife and daughter of whaling men, had a grandmother, Christian Noble, from the fishing village of Broadsea by Fraserburgh, who also "had shares in the whaling stations at Greenland."

By the middle of the 19th century, when the Moray Firth ports entered the whaling and sealing trade, whaling ships were often sealing first and only then heading for the whaling grounds of the Greenland Seas or the Davis Straits. Their initial destination in Davis Straits was Pond's Bay, where the whales were expected to gather in the middle weeks of July, and hunting should be good, as soon as the ice released its grip.

The whale ship would sail to the hunting grounds, and the master would send a good man aloft to the crow's nest to seek out the quarry. As soon as he saw a whale, or a 'fish' he would shout out, the boats would be lowered and would race to the place where the whale, or its spout, was seen. In the early days the harpooner would throw his harpoon, but by the mid 1850s most boats had a harpoon gun in the bows, and that would be aimed and fired at the whale instead. The harpoons were not intended to kill, but to act as a giant fish hook, with the boat and crew acting as the rod.

The boatsteerer was in charge until the boat was within harpoon range. He steered the boat to approach the whale from the quarter, taking care to avoid the flukes of the tail that could overturn a boat or reduce it to splinters in a second. Once close enough, the harpooner would throw the harpoon overhand, usually two handed, and ensure it stuck into the body of the whale. If the harpooner was a good shot and hit the whale, that boat would raise a flag, a 'jack' to signal the mother ship he is 'fast' to the whale. According to Surgeon Trotter of *Enterprise*, once the jack is raised, 'the whole ship resounds with the cry "a fall, a fall' and…Every man rushes on deck in an instant, some new out of bed and half naked, some with a bundle of clothes in their hand… all jump into the boats." The other boats would then race over and try and add their harpoon to that of the first, the 'fast' boat.

Once struck the whale would take off, either diving or driving through the water or ice, dragging the small boat behind it. Naturally the extra weight tired the animal, and if more than one boat managed to thrust in its harpoon, then the whale would tire the quicker.

In theory killing a whale was a very cold-blooded exercise, but it was not always one sided as the whale often put up a tremendous struggle that could carry a small boat miles from its mother ship. A whale could dive headfirst or thrash with its tail or could overturn a careless boat with a flick of its flukes, or a flap of its fins if the boat is broadside on.

William Barron in page 73 of his book *Old Whaling Days* mentioned a 'diabolical whale' that waited until the hunters were close then 'she would strike out with her tail and fins in a vicious manner.' Sometimes the whale won the fight and survived. The harpoon might slip free of the flesh, or the line may become tangled and have to be cut, or the whale might take all 60 or 70 fathoms of line and swim away, particularly if only one boat was fast. If that happened then the jack was lowered and the master of the whaling ship would be an unhappy man.

The whale usually swam away at around five or seven knots, dragging the boat or boats, behind it. It was common for a whale to drag out all 600 fathoms of a boat's lines, or those of two or more boats. Whales cannot breathe underwater so must surface, and when it did, other boats would add their harpoons and the whale would run again, but each time it surfaced the boats would be waiting. When it eventually stopped in sheer exhaustion, loss of blood and pain, the boats would close for the kill with lances. They approached with caution, for the whale could still be dangerous. They would thrust lances into its body to kill it, and then tow the dead body home.

The most immediately fatal thrust was into the narrow throat, fifteen inches or so behind the blow-hole. Other vulnerable spots were below the fins and forward toward the throat and below the fin and toward the heart. If the whale spouted blood through its blow hole, then it was mortally wounded and the boats pulled back and left it to die.

The hunt and kill was an exhilarating but bloody business, but every whale killed meant more oil money for the crew, and so less worry about poverty during the winter. The whale hunters, like the seal hunters, were doing a job and making money to feed their families the best way they could. They could not afford to be sentimental about their quarry, and to judge by the journals and diaries that they left, few were. Hunting and killing were among the prime sports of the Victorian era, and whale hunting combined sport with profit.

By the 1850s the whaling masters were beginning to bewail the lack of quality harpooners. They recalled days when daring harpooners would leap onto the back of a whale to ensure a secure fix, but such men were now rare. It is possible that this occurred because the masters and owners were concentrating more on sealing, which did not give men the opportunity of gaining the requisite experience. By the 1850s some harpooners did not even manage to hit the whale, either through lack of skill or lack of nerve. It must have been daunting to approach such a huge animal, knowing the inherent danger of being capsized with the attendant risks of frostbite and losing a limb or even dying. The *Banffshire Journal* mentioned one occasion when a Peterhead whaling master became so frustrated at seeing his harpooners miss their target that he threatened to fire on the next boat to fail. Alexander Trotter mentioned a failed attempt when "several bottle nosed whales very near us. One of our boats tried to get one of them but unfortunately the harpooner missed it."

When the whale was eventually killed, the boats tied a line to its tail to tow it back to the ship. If the fish has swum a long distance this journey could take some back breaking hours, but the men might still have sung a shanty, knowing that they have succeeded in gaining oil money.

When they reach the ship, the whale's head was removed and the specktioneer took off the whalebone. After that the blubber was stripped away, kept for a couple of days then stored in the special tanks or in casks. When the last useful or profitable parts were removed from the whale, what remained, known as the kran, was cut away.

Estimates of the amount of oil a large sized whale could supply, but a whale of about 65 feet could bring at least nine tuns, with the smaller fish proportionally less. A large whale could have blubber as much as fifteen inches thick, but twelve was more common, and sometimes the layer was only of eight inches. Either way, flensing, (or flinching) the whale, stripping it of its blubber, was a happy time on board. The more whales were flensed, the more profit the ship had made and the fatter would be the pay packet of the men.

Whaling was dangerous in many ways. As well as the risk of the small whaling boats being lost in the ice or in fog, there was the possibility of being overturned by a whale, or of the entire ship foundering. There was also the worry of snow blindness, or the always-present fear of accident from falling from the yards. Life at sea was always hazardous.

When the whaling ship arrived back in port, the blubber was taken to the boiling yards to be made into oil. The process was simple. Whale blubber was boiled alone in a huge copper pan, and seal blubber with water added. The blubber was boiled for a few hours and the resulting liquid, the oil, run into large troughs, or coolers. There it lay until the sediment sunk. The remainder was poured into casks and was ready for sale. The profits could be large, with oil in the later 1850s at over £40 per tun, whalebone at from £300 to £550 per ton and sealskins fetching as high as 7/6 (37.5p) each in a good year.

By the early 1850s, the Moray Firth ports were wakening to the profits that could be made in the north. The men who hoped to invest in a whaling or sealing ship would research their market and find out exactly what was involved in Arctic seafaring.

Chapter Three

A TYPICAL WHALING VOYAGE

I did not like the whale fishing. There is no sight for the eye of the inquisitive after the first glance and no variety to charm the mind. Desolation reigns around: nothing but snow, or bare rocks and ice.
John Nicol, Mariner, page 61

There was no typical whaling voyage, for every trip depended on various factors such as the weather, the composition of the crew, the ship herself, the character and experience of the ship's master and, probably as important, luck. However, there were certain events that were common to most voyages, and although the number of logbooks and journals of whaling ships are limited, what occurred in one vessel may be reasonably accepted as being an example of what could occur in others.

The historian is fortunate that there are surviving sources for whaling voyages, although these are scattered, belonging to many ports. In one particular aspect, whalers were different from other British merchant vessels, for the law obliged them to carry a surgeon. In many cases this man was young, either a recently qualified doctor, or a medical student, and these men frequently kept a diary or journal of their experiences.

Before they left port, the ship's agent would pay the Greenlandmen an advance on their wages, normally a month's pay which was in theory to buy suitable clothing for the voyage. This practice was common for seamen throughout Britain. For example in Leith in 1837, "The owners came on board and payed each man one month advance"

The Greenlandmen would also sign 'articles' or a contract for the forthcoming season but would not receive the bulk of their wages until all the seal and whale blubber had been boiled into oil and sold off and the amount due to each man was calculated. The thought of that final pay day would sustain the Greenlandmen throughout the rigours of the voyage, for a bumper pay meant they could roar through the taverns of Banff or Fraserburgh, or in whatever fishing village that they returned to.

The whaling ship would leave her homeport around February or March, usually to the accompaniment of cheers and good wishes from a healthy crowd of family and friends. From Scotland, the ship would head for Shetland or Orkney to complete the crew with the splendid and relatively cheap, seamen from the northern isles, and then would head north. The shipmasters liked the men from Shetland, as Hector Adams of Victor said in 1877: "The Shetland hands were sober and clean, well supplied with good clothing ... and steady old lads they were." When Gordon Stables sailed north in *Vulcan* as a first year medical student, he mentioned taking on extra hands, stores and woollen clothing at Lerwick, and left to cheers from the other seamen and women in small boats.

Even this early part of the voyage could be uncomfortable for those unaccustomed to the sea, with surgeon Trotter, at all of twenty years old, writing: "I kept my bed all this day, being sick." The numbers of sealing and whaling vessels calling at Lerwick could be surprising, with Trotter reporting: "I suppose there are about 40 lying in Lerwick harbour all around us." In some cases, at least in Stromness in Orkney, the bellman would patrol the town, clanging his bell and telling the crew that their vessel was due to depart.

Until the introduction of steam power, the ship had a choice. It could seal hunt and then return direct to Scotland, or seal hunt and then head for the whaling grounds. The system changed around 1860, when steam power gave some vessels the capability to go sealing and return home, dropping off their extra hands, before sailing for a second voyage to the whaling grounds.

The period of sealing and whaling from the Moray Firth straddled this divide, with the industry beginning in 1852 and lasting until the late 1860s. However all the vessels from Nairn, Banff and Fraserburgh were sail powered, so either sailed exclusively for the sealing, or made a single voyage, sealing first and then whaling. To some extent, the advent of steam power marked the beginning of the demise of Fraserburgh's involvement in the trade.

Leaving Shetland or Orkney, the sealing ships would sail to Jan Mayen or Spitsbergen for the seals, but would hunt or shoot just about anything they encountered. Surgeon Trotter's journal provides ample proof of this constant preoccupation with killing for sport. On the 7th of March 1856 he "managed to get out of bed and on deck for near an hour and shot a gull from the stern." Six days later he wrote that he "shot four gulls last night … perhaps a cruel proceeding, but in such matters ones conscience is easily pacified. They are called by the sailors malleys or molly ducks … I have shot about a hundred … since leaving Shetland." Stables spoke of "this dreary season of the year' as they sailed 'into a sea of darkness and desolation' that created a 'feeling on board was one of depression."

The weather was a constant danger, either with storms or, further north, fog and ice. Surgeon Trotter described one squall on the passage north from Shetland when the weather became "worse and worse, tremendous sea and frequent squalls of wind. Went on deck and saw a splendid though fearsome sight; the sea was almost entirely one mass of foam and the waves a tremendous size." Stables spoke of "the sun hidden behind such banks of rolling cumulus as I had never seen before … the seas were very high and green and seemed to play pitch and toss with the poor old *Vulcan*."

As if to compensate for the hardships, the northern seas could be astoundingly beautiful and full of interest. There were also deceptions, such as the times when Barron spoke of the mirage of a ship, "inverted in the air and with its masts touching … other times ships could appear elongated or stumpy … the clouds near the horizon to the northward appeared so much like the land with its snow-capped mountains that any … person might … be deceived, although we knew the land to be about 110 miles distant." Beauty could also be a forewarning of trouble, however, as when Barron mentioned witnessing the aurora borealis, followed by a northerly swell "which warned us to prepare for a gale." There was also comfort within the ship as Stables mentions: "down below in the cabin … when the big lamp was lit, and a splendid fire roaring in the great stove, over which shimmered a brass coffee urn… I did not think it half unpleasant."

When the vessels reached the ice the reason for the double planking and reinforced bow would soon be apparent. Here is Trotter again. On 17 March 1856: "we came to large masses of ice, floating about in streams, through which we forced our way, the good ship getting many knocks and shaking at times."

Despite the strength of the ships, they could also let in water. *Vulcan* leaked, so the men were constantly at the pumps and their beds were wet despite their adding sheets of brown paper between the blankets for extra warmth. Men caught the cold and pneumonia as they sailed for the north. However, whaling ships tended to feed their men well. Gordon Stables spoke of "huge sides of beef" hung up in the fore and main tops and remaining frozen all through the voyage. The steward often had to saw the frozen meat with a saw, while the locker of Bass's beer in the cabin of *Vulcan* was always frozen, despite being near the cabin stove. Coffee was often preferred to beer or spirits, for even then, Arctic seamen knew that spirits were not warming in high latitudes.

The weather could change very suddenly in the north. Stables spoke of a time he was in his cabin playing the fiddle when he heard the mate thumping his boot three times on the deck, which was a signal for all hands on deck. Even before the men could muster, a sudden squall thrust *Vulcan* onto her beam ends so the sea surged over the deck, down the companion and surged into the cabin. Stables spoke of seas "higher than the maintop," which prefaced three weeks of gales that had the brig lying-to as she was driven westward into the Atlantic. That storm tore *Vulcan*'s sails, carried off her job-boom, damaged her winch and damaged her bulwarks.

The weather on the voyage north could vary. Vulcan experienced snow showers that laid a white carpet on deck, with men using crowbars to chip it away. Taking off protective mittens was to risk frostbite. Working aloft on icy ropes was hazardous; men's breath froze on the bunks in which they slept and on the bulwarks of the forecastle to form a film of ice. There was always the risk of accidents. Vulcan lost her crow's-nest; it slipped down the mast, bringing the occupant, elderly Kenny McKenzie with it and breaking his leg. He recovered from that, but was again injured when the vessel was stove by ice two months later.

Although the ships were far from home, they were frequently in company with other sealers and whalers: on the 24 March 1856 Trotter mentioned he: "counted no less than 31 vessels…nearly half of them…were Norwegians, Danes and Dutchmen." It was also common practice for masters or surgeons to pay their neighbours a visit. Trotter again, on 22nd March: "the captain of the brig *Sovereign* of Fraserburgh came on board and stayed until 1 o' clock."

Sighting the ice blink was always a major event for the whaling or sealing ships. The ice blink was a bright light above the horizon, created by the reflection of the pack ice on the sky. It signified that the vessel had reached the hunting grounds and the killing could commence. There were different types of ice on the passage north, from slush, to 'streams' of ice, which were areas of small pieces of floating ice that rattled against the hull in a never ending cacophony of sound. The man in the crow's- nest was constantly on the lookout for more dangerous, larger icebergs, or the thin bay ice, the round pancake ice or the infinitely larger pack ice that extended toward the pole. When the vessel reached the pack ice, she would cruise the edge, searching for seals, spotting the occasional bear that might be shot, and hoping for whales. The pack ice could be just a plateau of ice, stretching forever into the unseen horizon, but it could also disguise numberless channels of sea, hummocks of ice, 'pussy holes' used by the seals for breathing, and huge packs of seals.

The actual seal hunting was an ugly business, but when the Greenlandmen had killed or 'captured' enough, the ship would either return home or go onto the whaling. At all times there was the risk of being stuck in the ice. *Enterprise* experienced this in April 1856: "On going on deck this morning about 8 o'clock I found we were sticking fast among large masses of ice and unable to move." Even when the ice was absent, there could be storms, such as the one of 16 April 1856 that burst the foresail of *Enterprise*, or the combination of gales, fogs and icebergs that endangered her on the 23rd of that same month.

Sealing continued at every opportunity, with everything living they encountered liable to be killed, but there was still time for the Mayday ceremony. This affair seems to have been peculiar to the seal and whaling men, but was similar to the Crossing the Line ceremony of seamen in more southern latitudes. Stables reported that on that day *Vulcan* was decorated with a garland of ribbons Composed of ribbons handed to the seamen from their wives and girlfriends, the garland was intended to bring luck to the voyage. The hands enjoyed a special dinner and extra rum.

Neptune, presumably one of the older hands, arrived in the evening, looking for "any of my boys?" By that he meant Greenmen, hands that had never been in the Arctic before. Men who presented Neptune with a bottle of rum were let off, but those who had no rum were shaved and ducked in a cheerful rout that was followed by dancing and fun. This type of ceremony was common to Greenland ships, for instance in the Dundee ship *Thomas* in 1834: "at 8 o'clock pm the ship was quiet except the rumour of shaving those who had never been at the Straits" and the following morning "bell rung as a sign of the approaching Neptune with his comrade." Barron also mentioned the ceremony, with Greenmen "treated to a shaving, with the lazy lathered with coal tar and… powdered with crushed chalk and resin. After the shaving a few songs were sung."

Sometimes there was a more brutal celebration of the day. In *Enterprise* in the 1856 season, the ceremony was particularly unpleasant. Neptune and his wife arrived on board shortly after midnight, clad mainly in sealskin and put the Greenmen through a variety of painful and humiliating ordeals including setting fire to their beards and shaving them with a serrated blade that drew blood.

In the quiet periods, the Greenlandmen would amuse themselves in any way they could. Christian Watt of Broadsea, whose father, husband and brother all sailed to the Arctic, wrote that her father was "a grand fiddler, in the long weary hours at the whaling in the Arctic, he would play in the hours off duty; he was good at bagpipe music on the fiddle."

Success on the voyage depended on how many seals or whales they killed. A good 'capture' meant a profitable voyage, while a poor season meant low wages for the men and a bitter winter for their families. A bad voyage for the Dundee ship *Terra Nova* in 1896 indirectly led to the murder of Elizabeth Leggat by her embittered whaler husband, Richard. With no thought of wildlife conservation until much later in the century, the hunters killed thoughtlessly, believing that their prey was never ending. It is unlikely that they could foresee a day when seals or whales were scarce in the north.

When a whale was killed and towed back to the ship, the blubber was stripped off or 'flensed,' with the officers again earning their extra money. The harpooners removed any skin and cut the blubber into blocks, which the steersman reduced to a more manageable size before tossing them down a canvas chute to the linemanager in the hold. Once in the hold they were stuffed into casks. This last could be a dangerous business with the combination of gasses and a combined space.

It was the master's duty to decide when to return. If he thought there were no more seals or whales to catch, the ship was full or the weather too bad to continue, he would head home. Ultimately, it was on the whaling captain that the success or failure of the voyage depended, and it says much for the ship masters of Fraserburgh and, to a lesser extent, Banff, that the same men commanded their vessels for many years.

With messages exchanged with other vessels throughout the voyage, any returning ship carried news of the others in the ice. Sometimes the news was false, as in 1859 when the Dundee whaler *Narwhal* informed the people of Fraserburgh that their vessel *Melinka* was lost in the ice. The news must have been devastating to the families, but the relief when *Melinka* eventually turned up would have been equally overwhelming.

When a vessel came home, hundreds of people would crowd to the harbour to witness its safe return, and the joy on the quayside can be imagined. Probably the nearest equivalent today would be the return of a military unit from a theatre of war. For the married men there would be the delight at reunification with their wives and families, while the unattached would contemplate splashing out their money in the pubs and taverns.

The ships' owners and shareholders, of course, would be the true winners as they divided the profit between them for ultimately, whaling and sealing was a business with wealth making the ultimate aim.

Chapter Four

THE SEALING TRADE

> *A fight was put a stop to by the Master interfering this afternoon. The bullies were our second mate and a seaman*
> John Wanless 01 Aug 1834: Journal of a Voyage to Baffin Bay aboard the ship *Thomas*

While Scottish vessels had hunted in the north since the early 1750s, seal hunting had been secondary to the pursuit of whales. That was not to say that sealing had not been important to British Arctic vessels. *Hawke* of London captured 250 seals in 1765, *North Star* of Dunbar 850 in 1783 and *Duke of York* of London a massive 5500 in 1774, but not until 1803 did Hope of Peterhead specialise in whale hunting. Other vessels followed Hope's lead, with *Enterprise* capturing 760 in 1806 and *Active* 2,500 in 1819. Three decades later Captain Martin's *Victor* of Peterhead killed 12,494 and gained 158 tuns of oil in a three-month voyage. Other ports took note of Peterhead's success, realised that seal hunting was easier than whaling, with less risk and nearly as much profit, and investors were soon clamouring to buy shares in seal-hunting companies. The Moray Firth seal and whale industry had been born.

There were many similarities between the sealing and whaling trades, and frequently a vessel was equipped for both seal and whale hunting, with the same master and crew.

After coming home in the summer or autumn of the previous year, the hunting vessels were laid up for the winter, and often repaired from the damage done to them by the ice and storms of the north. About the middle of January work began on fitting them out for the seal and whale hunting, with generally the smaller vessels fitted only for sealing and the larger for both. After some heartfelt leaving celebrations in the ports, the vessels sailed about the middle of February. Those ships that were sailing only for the Davis Straits whaling grounds would leave about a month later.

At this time a typical sealing voyage from any of the Moray Firth ports would last around three months, and there would be a crowd at the quayside to cheer off the departing vessel and wish them luck. Departure was an emotional time, with wives and sweethearts often in tears as they said farewell to the husbands, lovers and sons they would not see for months and maybe not at all. However they also knew that a successful voyage meant a more comfortable winter to come. Sometimes the farewells could be protracted as Matthew Campbell wrote about the departure of the Dundee vessel *Nova Zembla* in 1884: "We did not get up steam… till 12.30 PM as our crew were not all on board, they being mostly engaged in taking their leave of their families and bidding them adieu. In one case this took about an hour."

The sealing and whaling ships would stop at Shetland or Orkney to pick up extra hands. There were two reasons for this augmentation to the crew. Firstly the seamen of the northern isles were skilful and often experienced, and secondly, they seem to have been paid less. The *Banffshire Journal* of the 24th February 1852 says that "their labour, while it is of course cheap, is at the same time valuable." The Shetlanders were said to have called the time when the whalers were present 'the Greenland time' and the employment of many men would certainly give a valuable boost to the Shetland economy.

Although the seal and whale fishermen were known as Greenlandmen and the local newspapers said they were bound for Greenland, in reality they were more likely to hunt around the coasts of Jan Mayen Land or Spitsbergen, islands in the Greenland Sea rather than the island of Greenland itself. The ship would be provisioned for a longer period than three months in case of delays in the ice. It would take the sail-powered vessels about a month from leaving the Moray Firth to reach the seal fishing grounds, and after that the slaughter began.

The hunters knew that the female seals came on to the ice to pup after the middle of March, around the 18th to the 25th, and remained there until the pups were weaned. If the ice was unbroken, the hunters would simply wait and kill the seals as they emerged from pussy holes. There was nothing sporting about this procedure; the larger seals were shot, the younger clubbed to death with the ferocious seal clubs, or seal picks as they were sometimes known. Stables mentions *Vulcan* being virtually deserted, with only the master, cook, steward and a boy left on board. All the others were on the ice, hunting the seals, working two-by-two in case one man falls through a pussy hole or between two floes into deep water. There was fear, justified or not, of being dragged under by a shark. As the men hunted, Captain Stephen of *Vulcan* watched them through a telescope from the crow's-nest, and directed them to shoals of seals as best he could. The steward kept the captain warm with hot coffee.

If the ice was broken, the sealers hunted from the boats. They rowed the boats around the edges of the ice floes with a harpooner in the bows firing at the seals on the ice. This killing could sometimes be dangerous for the hunters as one species of seal, known as bladdernoses, were liable to fight back. These large animals could pull three or four men across the ice as the hunters attacked it with clubs. They could also throw a hunter into the icy water. The more common 'saddle' seals were easier to kill and rarely fought back. In the case of *Vulcan* at least, the officers carried rifles.

The sealers' prime objective was saddleback seals, so named because of the broad black band that extended from the back of the neck down either side. The young seals, or pups, were completely white, and it was not unknown for seal hunters to wait until they were fully suckled and had attained their maximum weight before killing them. Bladdernoses were less liked. These were the Hood seals, the males of which had a bag of loose skin on top of its head. If the bladdernose was attacked or in any way annoyed, the bag enlarged to around the size of a football. Unlike the saddlebacks, the bladdernose males would fight to defend its mate, either out of devotion, or from sheer pugnacity.

In a good season the hunters could come across a pack of seals that could be four miles broad and stretch as far as the eye could see. It was not unknown for two or more vessels to be fishing the same pack of seals but be out of sight of each other. Given such numbers it is not surprising that there seemed no limit to the possible success of the sealers; they could not imagine such a bounty ever ending, or their constant slaughter eroding the seal numbers to such an extent that they became an endangered species. The Victorian mind seems to have been incapable of such a thought process.

The hunters were primarily after the young seals, born in March or April and easy prey for men with clubs. According to the Banffshire Journal of 24 February 1852, the seal pups "became very fat during the period of suckling' and were then 'deserted by the mother and left to shift for themselves." As the young seals are reluctant to take to the water and catch fish, they remained on the ice, gradually losing weight until hunger drove them to swim. For the seal hunters then, the best time to kill the young seals was just as the mother left them, around the 8th of April, they believed, and until around the 15th. Therefore, sealing vessels would quite cold bloodedly watch and wait until the mother seal had weaned her pup before landing on the ice to hunt. After the 15th the young pups would get thinner and would lose their value.

There was no mercy and no sentiment, merely profit driven slaughter. The Victorians delighted in hunting for its own sake, with 'game bags' to record the number of animals, birds or fish that were pursued and exterminated in the pursuit of pleasure, for instance, as Trotter recorded on the 11th June 1856: "I shot a bird nearly all white with black legs called a snowbird by the sailors … is truly a beautiful creature."

With an attitude that saw stuffed animals used as ornaments in drawing rooms throughout the country, there was no thought of squeamishness in the killing of seals. It was a business, nothing more. Trotter describes the killing of the first seal: "one of the men shooting her from the boat and then another running onto the piece of ice and striking her on the head…with…a seal club. I was astonished at the immense quantity of blood."

The seal hunters seemed to have been surprised when the male seals tried to fight back, but had no qualms about using rifle or club in a bloody slaughter. In common with other sealing vessels, *Felix* of Banff had a large numbers of such things, described by the *Banffshire Journal* of 24 February 1852 as "ugly looking weapons quite calculated to end the life of any seal that may be foolish enough to stand up in defence of his hearth." A report of December 1858 in the same newspaper said the clubs were "not unlike the ancient battle axe." On the 26 March 1856 Trotter describes one as "rather like a pick than a club. It consists of a long wooden shaft and an iron head having a sharp point and certainly it appears to be well suited for the work it has to perform."

The young pups were around the size of a collie dog or even smaller and sat on the ice without trying to escape until they were clubbed to unconsciousness or death. Stables describe a hunt in sickening detail: "one blow from the sharp end of the club, and the baby is weltering in its gore. The skinning takes place immediately, and often pieces of the dark and quivering flesh… often the baby is only partially stunned, and when flayed may be seen to roll in agony on the snow." Some Fraserburgh seamen threw living but partially skinned seals into the sea to see if they would swim, or stamped on a baby so its cries attracted the mother, who would be shot. Polar bears often watched, but did not interfere.

When the seals eventually left the ice and took to the water, the hunters believed that the old seals headed north and the young seals south. After this first period of hunting, the sealing ships normally also headed northward in the wake of the larger, older seals that were harder to kill but which yielded a correspondingly greater amount of blubber and therefore profit. April or May were the favoured months for this stage of the hunt.

If the hunters were successful in capturing the old seals early in the season, they reckoned that it took the blubber of forty to make a tun of oil, but if they were captured later in the season when they had lost weight, it would need as many as seventy for a tun. Young seals averaged between 90 or 100 to the tun. When the sealing season was at its height, a successful ship could kill up to 600 mature and 2000 young seals. To get an idea of the extent of the slaughter, there were thirty-three vessels departing from Scotland alone in 1853. If each vessel caught only half the number of seals required for a successful season, it would amount to a total of 42,900 seals killed by Scottish vessels alone. If non-Scottish vessels, English, Dutch and German were added, the annual total would be frightening.

If the hunters had to travel far from the mother ship, the captured seals still had to be dragged on board by using what was often referred to as a 'lowery tow,' a one-inch rope ten feet long, and after the slaughter came the skinning. The skin and blubber were peeled off. The blubber on young seals was two or three inches thick, while on the old seals it was around four inches. Referring to Captain Hay of the Banff vessel *Felix* as the source, the *Banffshire Journal* of 24 Feb 1852 states that after being stripped of their skin and blubber, some of the old seals were put back in the water and "have been known to swim for some distance." As Stables also mentions this practise, it may have been common. The unthinking cruelty of skinning a live animal, yet alone placing it in freezing salt water immediately afterwards, was not mentioned.

The hunters usually took off the skin and blubber together and would drag both to the ship. This could be hard work if the men had travelled far, for an averagely strong man could only drag the skin of one old or three young seals at any one trip. If the hunting scene was six or seven miles across the ice from the ship, then the Greenlandmen had a long days' work to drag all their captures to be stored. Normally the skins were packed *in situ* then dragged over the ice. Given the distance and labour required in always bitter and sometimes foggy conditions, this was slow and laborious work.

Seal hunters had to be fast. If they came across a pack of seals they had to attack right away, in case the entire quarry escaped. It was not unknown for the seals to be killed, only for the ice to break and the entire capture to fall into the sea and be lost.

Once on board, the skin and blubber were separated in a process known as flensing or flinching. The Greenlandman would lay the skin over a sloping board, a flinching or flensing board, and use a sharp skinning knife to cut the blubber from the skin. Experience and accuracy were valuable here, as the skins would later be sold and if they were cut or mutilated they would fetch less money. The skins would then be stored in the hold.

The blubber was usually packed in casks in the sealing vessel, to be later boiled down into the valuable oil. Later vessels had a built in tank for the same purpose. If the supply of casks ran out, which could happen on a successful voyage, the blubber would be kept loose in the hold. Seal oil could be sold for between £25 and £35 per tun, and, like whale oil, would be used for lighting or lubrication. In a sale of whale and seal oil at Peterhead in October 1853, merchants from Newcastle, Leith, Aberdeen and Dundee paid £36 a tun for whale oil and £33 10/- for seal oil, with the entire cargoes of the ships being bought within the hour. Given the much more dangerous and longer voyage required to hunt whales than seals, the slight difference in price would encourage seal fishing; investors would be more likely to put their money into the safer trade.

As well as the oil, the skins of the seal could also be sold. Sealskin would usually be tanned and used for shoe making, or dressed and used as an exotic covering for trunks or similar items. Even in relatively modern times there was a market for little cuddly baby seal ornaments made from real sealskin.

Those vessels that hoped to also try the Greenland Seas whale hunting would leave the sealing grounds around the 10th of May, but for those who hoped for the longer trip and richer fishing of the Davis Strait, the 1st of May was the preferred date. The vessels which were fitted out only for sealing, or which were fortunate enough to have filled their holds, would head back to Scotland as the sealing season drew to a close.

Chapter Five

THE SEALING INDUSTRY OF NAIRN AND BANFF

For a time the gulls and skuas kept us company but they at last said farewell
Gordon Stables; 1859

Although the ports of the Moray Firth are spread over a large geographical area, it was only those of the southern or north facing coast that were tempted into the seal and whaling trade. Nairn, Banff and Fraserburgh entered the sealing trade nearly simultaneously, but with vastly differing fortunes. While Nairn's encounter was as brief as a summer's kiss, Banff had a short, intense and brilliant flirtation with the Arctic. Fraserburgh, however, built up a respectable fleet, but toning down to a comfortable and manageable relationship with the north that endured for almost two decades.

As well as these three ports, other places along the north-facing coast of the Moray Firth had a brief glance at the sealing industry. In 1852 there were hopes of a sealing company in Macduff and also in Inverness. Although the Macduff proposal never got beyond the discussion stage, a combination of merchants from Inverness and Garmouth purchased the 142-ton *Ranger*, which was built in 1836 and sailed as a successful sealer from Peterhead. The Garmouth company of Alexander Young and Company had built *Ranger*, which increased the Moray Firth connection.

Hugh Mann of Nairn was also tempted by the opportunities in the north. Hugh Mann was a 34 year old married shipowner, the son of James Mann, a farmer of Meadowfield at Auldearn. His younger brother John was the local harbourmaster. Mann fitted out the 5 year old, 98 ton *Lady Campbell* for the seal fishing, put Captain Cameron in command and filled her with a crew that included some experienced Arctic mariners. Unfortunately she was hardly out when she put into Aberdeen for repairs instead, but emerged too late for the season and instead sailed to Riga in the Baltic.

In February 1854 she tried again, but sailed from Aberdeen straight into the teeth of a North Westerly gale. The weather proved too much for her and the unfortunate *Lady Campbell* had hardly rounded Kinnaird Head when she had to put into Fraserburgh for further repairs. She sailed again and reached Lerwick on the 16th March, leaky and with an unhappy crew that refused to sail further north. After spending over £800 on *Lady Campbell*, the owners sold her by auction at the Saddle Inn in Sunderland. That was the end of Nairn's abortive experiment with the sealing trade, and left only Banff and Fraserburgh to carry the Moray Firth banner north.

Today it is difficult to imagine Banff as a European trading port. The harbour is small and in poor weather, heavy seas batter against the rocky shore to the west, while surf streams in to the beach that separates the town from its immediate neighbour, MacDuff. Nevertheless, whaling ships of the mid nineteenth century were not huge, and improvements had created what was then quite a comfortable harbour.

Founded as a port on the west side of the River Deveron, Banff has a long association with the sea. Favoured, or otherwise, with a visit by King Malcolm IV in 1163, the town never quite grew into a major commercial centre, but neither was it negligible, trading with the Hanseatic League in the middle ages and having King Robert I raise it to the status of a Royal Burgh in 1324. The River Deveron was liable to silting, so despite work in 1625 when the area of Guthrie's Haven, now the inner basin, was cleared of rocks, further improvements were necessary.

In 1770 John Smeaton, who was busy all over Scotland at that time, was commissioned to create a more modern harbour. In 1818 the even more famous Thomas Telford was responsible for the Lighthouse Quay, which gave Banff its outer harbour. Unfortunately, like most harbours along Scotland's east coast, entry depended on the state of the tide, so vessels would have to wait in the bay until conditions were suitable.

Banff's first flirtation with the whaling trade was in 813, when, according to the Second Statistical Account, "a Greenland whale fishing company was formed and two vessels fitted out." In 1814 *Earl of Fife* of Banff, commanded by Captain Wilson caught 17 whales, with 135 tons of oil, and the following year she caught 5 whales with 38 tons of oil. That year she was icebound in the Arctic, together with a large group of other whaling ships. The ice closed around her on the 19th May and the next day the lookout in the masthead reported no sign of clear water. She remained trapped until 21st June, when most of the ships struggled free. During these weeks *Earl of Fife* drifted from latitude 78 degrees to latitude 76. She sailed into Banff bay on 17 August, flying a signal 'All well- five fish.'

The following year *Earl of Fife* was lost. She was warped out of the harbour in the morning of 12 April 1816 on her way to the whaling grounds. At that stage the weather was mild, but as soon as she hit the open sea, the wind shifted and strengthened. After about an hour, it was obvious *Earl of Fife* could make no headway, and as it was unsafe to return to harbour, the captain ordered her to come to anchor. However about four o clock the following afternoon the anchor cables parted and she was driven onto the bar. Although the crew was saved, the ship was wrecked.

In most circumstances, the owners of a ship would apply to their insurance company, pick up the value and carry on business, but in this case the insurers proved sticky. John Smith and the other owners of *Earl of Fife* had insured her with three separate companies. One third of her value was insured with Lloyds of London, one third with Goodard of Leith and one third with Fraser of Aberdeen. While Lloyds paid up immediately, the two Scottish companies proved intractable and the ship's owners took them to the High Court of Admiralty. The underwriters first claimed that the owners should never have abandoned the vessel, and then said that the ship was badly equipped for the Arctic, and had hove to in the bay to await stores and that was the cause of her destruction.

The case came to court on the 2nd March 1818, with Henry Cockburn acting for the underwriters and Francis Jeffrey for the owners. The court decided *Earl of Fife* was fully equipped so the owners won their case.

The second Banff vessel was *Triad*, under Captain Slater. She seemed to have a slightly longer career, capturing 13 whales in 1813, with 120 tons of oil, 6 whales in 1815 with 59 tons of oil and 2 whales as late as 1818, with 16 tons of oil.

According to the Statistical Account, the company lost a lot of money from their venture into whaling, but by the early 1850s Banff had recovered her confidence and was ready to try the northern fisheries again. Presumably encouraged by Peterhead's success in the sealing trade, a seal fishing company was formed in Banff in the autumn of 1851, with Thomas Adam as one of the leading members. According to the 1851 Census, there was a Thomas Adam, bank agent, in Banff, so this was probably the same man. Adam was a local man, born in Banff in 1806 and married to Mary, with whom he had nine children. He lived in some style at 48 High Street, not far from the present Royal Bank of Scotland. His two servants proved he was of adequate means, but once again, a principal player in the sealing trade was a man with no seagoing experience.

Casting around for a suitable vessel, the company located and purchased *Felix*. At 91 tons, *Felix* was strong and handy and had a history of working in conditions every bit as extreme as those she would encounter at the sealing. Originally built by Sloan and Gemmell in Ayr to carry iron between Ardrossan in Ayrshire and Liverpool, Admiral John Ross had seen her when he was searching for shipping to take him to the Arctic to search for the missing explorer Sir John Franklin, and he purchased her immediately. Named *Felix*, after Sir Felix Booth, an English distilling magnate who helped finance Ross's expedition, the vessel survived the rigours of Ross's expedition, and so the Banff Sealing Company bought her at an auction at the Kings Arms Hotel, Ayr, in late 1851. The following year she was the smallest vessel to enter the sealing trade to date.

This new venture aroused great interest in Banff, so when *Felix* left harbour in the middle of February 1852, a large crowd had gathered to watch her sail. Some would be simply curious, but others would have friends and family on board and would naturally be apprehensive as they sailed north for the first time. According to the *Banffshire Journal*, of 24 February 1852 as *Felix* "turned her bow to the northwards, she was greeted with a loud burst of cheering."

Such scenes were common when the whaling and sealing vessels left for the north, with every town having its own ceremony. Worries ran deep, even in a community used to seafaring hazards.

The Banff Sealing Company had taken every possible precaution to prepare *Felix* for the voyage. Captain Hay was an experienced Arctic seaman who had sailed on previous sealing and whaling expeditions, and four of the eight hands they had were also experienced whalers. *Felix* would make up the remainder of her crew by taking on another fourteen men at Lerwick, some of whom, being Shetlanders, might also have whaling or sealing experience.

Although *Felix* herself was a strongly built vessel the company overhauled and strengthened her further, added four boats made by the local boat builder, Mr Watson and planned to add a further boat at Lerwick. They piled her with provisions, with 45 hundredweight of salted beef amongst the three tons of butcher meat for the crew. She also carried the carcass of an ox dangling aloft to ensure fresh meat, which must have given *Felix* a bizarre appearance as she left harbour. This method of carrying meat seems to have been not unusual among the Moray Firth sealers, for in May 1856 Trotter mentioned *Enterprise* with "fresh beef... hanging up in legs about the rigging." *Felix* also had bread and flour among the six months provisions, so even if she was unfortunate enough to be frozen in amongst the ice, the crew would be able to eat.

When she left Greenland, *Felix* was supposed to reach the seal fishing grounds in the middle of March and return to Banff late in May. She carried casks capable of holding 25 tuns of oil from the seal blubber, and space in her hold for another 55 tuns, which would give her a capacity of 80 tuns. Although she was intended primarily for sealing, she also carried harpoons and warps for whaling. As the *Banffshire Journal* boasted, 'at least four of her crew are excellent harpooners.'

It was common practise for any ship that returned from the seal or whale fishing to carry news of the remainder, for at a time when there was no radio, telegraph or any other form of instant communication, the long absences were a trial for those left behind. With whaling and sealing such a dangerous occupation, it would be hard not to dwell on the possibility of sunken ships and small boats lost in the ice. It was Captain John Stephen of the Fraserburgh sealer *Melinka* that carried first news of *Felix* when *Melinka* arrived home on the 13th May, and although she only said the vessel had been 'seen among the seals' even that scant news would have assured the wives and mothers that their men were still alive and making money.

Captain Stephen also reported that the 'weather was more boisterous than it had been for many preceding years' which contrasted with the mild spring in Scotland. As a reminder of the dangers of the trade, Stephen mentioned the loss of the Peterhead sealer *Joseph Green* of 353 tons, which was stove by the ice on the 20th March and sank with the loss of Captain Stewart and three of the crew. Such news would only make the wives of Banff more anxious for the return of their men.

That first voyage by a Banff vessel continued to create considerable interest in the town, to judge by the amount of column inches the *Banffshire Journal* expended. *Felix* arrived back in Banff late in May, and as well as having a successful voyage in the pursuit of seals, she also brought back the skin and head of a polar bear.

Bear hunting was a common pursuit of the Greenlandmen, and most journals have at least one mention of at least seeing a bear. When Christian Watt's father was sailing on *Brilliant* he shot a polar bear, and gave the skin to Lady Saltoun, the London based, elderly mother of the landowner. The local people knew her as 'Old Ness Madgie,' but it was significant that a local whaler thought highly enough of her to present her with tribute from the Arctic.

The attitude of Victorians to both landowners and wildlife contrasts vividly with what is today considered normal, and the newspapers gloried in aspects of hunting which would currently be thought terrible. Bears were considered fair game for the hunters, with Trotter mentioning on the 3rd June 1856: "we got 2 bears today. They were shot swimming in the water. One was young and the other was old" and a week later: "a bear was observed … and four or five of our men with loaded guns came to meet him."

Men aboard other vessels were just as avid hunters. In 1874 Thomas Macklin, aboard the Dundee whaler *Narwhal* wrote: "this morning before breakfast I went away with the second mate, bear shooting. We shot three…we were away from the ship forty minutes only. "It was said that in Peterhead, that the ship's master could claim the skin of any polar bear killed.

The *Banffshire Journal* gave detailed reports about the hunting of *Felix*'s bear. It seems that when the bear was first seen the hands were still seal hunting, so "an attack on Master Bruin was deferred until a later period." A few hours later the mate and two of the crew armed themselves with muskets and pikes and set out to hunt down the bear, purely for the sport.

After walking three miles across the ice, they approached "the monster, which was in size fully as large as an ordinary Aberdeenshire three-year old stot" the mate tried to fire, but the musket did not work, and instead the bear attacked them and the mate had to run. Placing a second percussion cap on his musket, he tried to shoot it again, hitting the bear in the head. Wounded but still alive, the bear jumped into the sea, but there was enough ice nearby for the seamen to follow, firing whenever they got the opportunity.

With the ice broken, the chase was nearly as dangerous for the sealers as it was for the bear, and they had to jump across chasms, or even use a small berg as a raft to cross a stretch of open water. After a further three miles they eventually came close enough for one of the hunters to thrust his pike into the bear's head. The pike snapped and the prey escaped again, with the iron pike head protruding from his skull. However the bear was now tiring and weakened from loss of blood. Trying but failing to regain the ice, it began to "swim more slowly." Afraid that the bear might die and sink in the water, the mate ran to the animal and, reaching from the ice, grabbed its ears. The bear opened its jaws and roared, whereupon the mate thrust a musket down the bear's throat and fired, killing the animal, and, according to the Banffshire Journal of 25 May 1852: "the monster was dragged upon the ship."

Such adventures seem to have been meat and drink to the men who sailed in the sealing ships. Even if we do not agree with their attitudes, there can be no doubting their spirit or courage. Not many people would willingly approach a wounded polar bear, yet alone grab hold of its ears.

With that first sealing season considered a success, the Banff Seal and Whale Fishing Company contemplated sending a second vessel out the following year. There was also speculation that a second company could be formed and talk of a sealing company in neighbouring MacDuff as well. It seemed that the Moray Firth ports were about to leap into the sealing in a big way.

However, nothing can ever be certain when dealing with the sea, and on the evening of the 19th September 1852, *Felix* was stranded just outside Banff harbour. What could easily have been a disaster was averted when a host of volunteers rushed forward to rescue her. Helping people in trouble at sea seems to have come naturally in that period, but Thomas Adam, on behalf of the owner, publicly thanked them and paid many who had freely given their muscle power.

With casks lashed alongside to keep her afloat, *Felix* was brought into the inner harbour to be inspected for damage. Quite possibly the owners believed that their venture into sealing was already over, but a thorough inspection found that *Felix* was as sturdy as they had originally hoped. There was damage to her bulwarks and 'false keel', much of the coppering was scraped away, and the planking of the hull was damaged, but not badly.

The copper sheath was there for protection against the teredo worm, a bivalve mollusc, usually known as ship worm that can grow to around three feet in length and bores holes in the hulls of wooden vessels. *Felix's* hull would be much stronger than most vessels, with a second or 'double' layer of planking in place and some vessels often had a 'trebling' or third layer at the bows, the part of the vessel that made initial and constant contact with the ice. Even with this strengthening, internal beams and ice plates, the number of vessels lost in the sealing and whaling was frightening, which makes it ironic that *Felix* should be damaged just outside her own port.

When the tide was suitable *Felix* was taken to the slip to be properly examined and repaired ready for the following year's sealing. The company was not yet ready to surrender their dreams of profit from the north.

More encouraged by the success of *Felix* at the sealing than discouraged by her misadventure outside the harbour, the Banff Seal and Whale Fishing Company invested in a second vessel when they bought *Alexander Harvey*, a barque of 292 tons that was to have a distinguished career. During the winter months the company readied her for the coming season by having her planking doubled and made suitable for the trade.

Both vessels sailed from Banff on the last Sunday of February 1853. After his successful season with *Felix*, Captain Hay was transferred to the larger *Alexander Harvey*, which was equipped for both sealing and whaling. Repaired and ready for a second season, *Felix* sailed under a

Captain Fraser, intended only to hunt for seals. *Alexander Harvey* was a major investment for Banff, one of the largest vessels to sail from the port. As an example, the largest of the fourteen vessels in Banff harbour on the 15th February 1853, was *Empress* at 359 tons, followed by *Alexander Harvey*, then *Minerva* at 284 tons, while the smallest was the 29-ton *Chance*. It is sometimes humbling to realise quite how small were the vessels in which seamen carried the trade of Britain less than two centuries ago.

Although the possibilities of profit were enticing, the Banff Seal and Whale Fishing Company were investing a fair chunk of capital in their venture. As well as the initial purchase price, there was the cost of double planking on a ship of *Alexander Harvey's* size. There was also the expense of bringing in whaling and sealing gear, provisioning the vessel for a voyage of uncertain length, and paying the crew. Indeed the company spent £6000 purely to purchase and fit out their two vessels, with *Alexander Harvey* costing twice the price of the smaller *Felix*. Much of the expenditure was in wages, for these sealing and whaling vessels had larger crews than others of a similar size. *Felix*, at only 91 tons, carried 24 men, and *Alexander Harvey* the same number, but added another 24 in Shetland. The crew would have been crammed into their quarters, adding to the discomfort of what would already have been an uncomfortable voyage.

The cost of food was also considerable, with a vessel of the size of *Alexander Harvey* carrying stores to the value of around £800, while *Felix* would carry half that amount. The local farmers would certainly profit from the large amounts of butcher meat carried by the Arctic vessels and doubtless the merchants of Banff would rub their hands in glee at the prospect of supplying the company. There may well have been money to be made in sealing, but the profit benefited more people than just the company shareholders.

Felix arrived back before the end of May with 11600 seals and about 14 tons of oil, while *Alexander Harvey* left the sealing grounds to hunt for whales. She arrived back toward the end of August, with huge crowds gathering on the quay to cheer her home. However, her venture at the whaling had not been successful, and although she brought home 1700 seal skins and 20 tuns of seal oil, this was not a vast amount. Probably as important to the gathered wives and mothers, the crew returned intact and healthy. She was not allowed to linger long in harbour however, for a week later she was readied for a voyage to the Baltic possibly with a cargo of herring. The sealing industry added substantially to the overall trade of the port of Banff for 1853.

In the coasting trade, Banff itself had a total of 308 vessels, at 18,443 tons coming inward, with 228 vessels at a total of 11,678 tons clearing outward. Of the 21 British vessels coming into the port in 1853, two were from the Greenland trade, at 383 tons from a total tonnage of 2,144. There were also 43 foreign vessels, with a total tonnage of 2,408. Outward bound for foreign ports were 21 British ships, with the two Greenland vessels accounting for 383 tons from the total of 1,256, and 53 foreign vessels at 4245 tons. Banff had good reason to feel proud of its growth, as the shipping tonnage was at its largest, with 13,009 tons for the 145 vessels belonging to the port. The shipping had doubled in ten years, and the trend seemed inclined to continue. The customs revenue had increased in proportion, with a 30% increase in the years 1853 to 1854 alone. With such figures, and a seemingly endless supply of raw material waiting on the Arctic ice, the owners and shareholders of the Banff Sealing and Whaling Company had every reason to view the future with optimism.

It was hardly surprising that the movements of the sealing vessels should be viewed with considerable interest by the townspeople. In most whaling centres, it was customary for the seamen of the fleet to celebrate before departure. In Peterhead this pre-voyage party was known as a 'foy' but in Banff they had a slightly different, and apparently more formal, method of saying goodbye. Before *Alexander Harvey* left for the 1854 season, there was a farewell supper and ball held in St John's Lodge, Seatown. A lot of thought and much preparation had gone into the event, with ship's flags decorating the hall and Mr Stewart of the Market Inn preparing the meal.

With the event starting at eight in the evening, more than sixty people attended, mainly the seamen from the Greenland vessels but also the great and good of Banff, with a Captain McDonald acting as chairman and Captain Fraser of *Alexander Harvey* the croupier. As was normal for any respectable Victorian event, Captain McDonald said grace first, and then told the assembled and possibly disappointed company that there would be no drinking after the supper. Before the meal, however, toasts were drunk to various people including the Earl of Fife, a major landlord of the area, and what the Journal termed 'the Enterprising Proprietors of the Whale Ships and the Captain of the *Harvey* and his Youthful Crew.'

The term youthful is interesting, signifying perhaps a lack of experience among the hands, or a hope for adventure rather than a steady occupation by veteran Greenlandmen. The dancing began after nine and lasted for ten hours nonstop, which says much for the stamina of the youthful crew, more for the endurance of their elders and a great deal for the enthusiasm of a ball in which there was no alcohol. In a very Victorian manner, Captain McDonald praised the seamen's behaviour during the evening and advised them to save their wages for their old age by putting any spare money in a savings bank. The seamen cheered him as he left, having spent the night in sober hilarity. It was time to return to the north with optimism and spirits on a high and hopes of a massive haul of seals. All that was needed was favourable weather and good luck.

After being delayed by a strong northerly gale, the two Banff vessels eventually left for the north, with *Felix* struggling out of the harbour on the 22nd and *Alexander Harvey* a few days later. The sea initiated them to the new season with a violent north westerly gale that raised massive waves as *Felix* headed first for Stromness in Orkney where she picked up fifteen more hands. Orkney and Shetland were always a reservoir of good quality seamen for the sealing and whaling ships, and although there are tales of some animosity between the men from the northern isles and those from the mainland ports, overall the two seem to have worked well enough together.

A Wild Rough Lot

Once they had completed their crew in the northern isles, the Banff vessels steered north, expecting to continue the successes of the previous two seasons. However, after all their high hopes, tragedy now struck the small sealing fleet of Banff. As was normal in those days, any ship returning from the north carried news of the others, so that anxious relatives could hear about their men. It was a Peterhead vessel called *Pomona* that first carried the news of the loss of *Felix,* and there would be sore hearts among the women on Banff as they waited for conformation. Captain Robertson's tale was brief and unsatisfactorily fragmentary. He merely reported that he had spoken to a foreign vessel that had picked up part of the *Felix*'s crew, but two had died on the ice.

Naturally there was speculation in Banff. If two men had died upon the ice, they may have been there for some time before they were rescued. Captain Robertson also said that the mate, a Peterhead man named Allan, and his son-in-law, Captain Hay were both missing. In a style typical of the practical Victorians, the *Banffshire Journal* reported that *Felix* "with her cargo and stores was worth upwards of £1300" and the "greater part was covered by insurance."

The same edition of the Journal also quoted Robertson as saying that the "season has been uncommonly stormy, rending the prosecution of the fishing both difficult and dangerous." He said that *Violet* of Hull had also been lost and his own ship had returned damaged, and with no "young ice to be seen the fishery had to be prosecuted in boats, which were often swamped by the heavy seas" *Pomona* had herself rescued a boat and crew of the Peterhead ship *Alert* which stormy seas had driven from the ship.

With the people of Banff anxious, more news gradually filtered south from the sealing grounds, and they learned exactly in what conditions their men were working. It had been an eventful season on the sealing grounds. A report from Hamburg told them that the English brig *Union* had been abandoned by her crew, but a party from a German vessel, *Joanna Mayen* boarded and carried her into port. A report from Lerwick said that the Scottish sealer *Gipsy* had been stove in but other vessels were busy among the seals. It was not until the 16th May, after two weeks of speculation that the *Banffshire Journal* could write the final story of *Felix*, under the heading "Suffering of a Sealer's Crew in the Arctic Seas."

By that time many of the crew had returned home, and their collective story brings the harrowing truth of a sealer's life. It is a sharp contrast to the speculative investment of would-be wealthy men, but a story of hardship, suffering and quiet courage by men who were working to feed their families.

Felix had arrived in the seal fishing ground on the 6th of April and was busily hunting among the ice when a southerly gale suddenly rose. The gale drove ice floes against the hull, and possibly damaged her rudder. Captain Hay ordered all sails except the main topsail lowered, but the helm did not answer and *Felix* was helpless. At nine in the morning the wind drove her onto an iceberg, damaging her severely despite her double planking; she began to take in water. Captain Hay ordered the crew to the pumps and began to throw away ballast to lighten the ship. They Greenlandmen fought to save *Felix* all that day, cutting away the foremast and main topmast to prevent her going down by the head but despite their efforts, in the evening *Felix* was waterlogged and heeled over on her side.

There was a moment of hope when a vessel appeared nearby, but although the crew signalled, there was no response. In a time before radios, distance was relative and a 91 ton vessel was small against the vastness of the Arctic. With the ship sinking and no help at hand, the crew had to abandon. Launching the boats, they made a final desperate effort to right *Felix* but she was too badly damaged and to remain on board was futile as well as dangerous. However, they had spent so long in trying to fight the inevitable that *Felix* was waterlogged, and the men had little chance to salvage anything before they took to the ice. Stepping into the open boats with only what they stood up in, they had little spare food, water or even extra clothing for the bitter cold of the Arctic.

The crew of *Felix*, twenty-six men, crammed into the open boats that bobbed around the northern seas with icebergs of various sizes looming out of the dark. They had left the ship in such haste that they had not even a compass and were exhausted and probably disheartened from their day of unrelenting labour.

There were a few moments of hope when they thought there was a white sail gleaming through the dark, but when they grabbed the oars and pulled toward it, they realized that the white sail was only a curiously shaped iceberg. Even more unfortunate, the long pull through the gloom had separated the crews, with the captain's boat racing ahead of the others. Cold, disappointed and divided, they sought a suitable iceberg on which to shelter for the remainder of the night. Without proper clothing, they spent a bitter night, and in the morning, after a meagre meal of bread, everybody tried to move toward the captain so they were at least together.

The ice floes had separated in the night and the captain's boat was far from the men, so they had to scramble and leap over cracks in the ice but eventually they reached the captain. However, there were two casualties, with James Burns from Banff and James Tours of Stromness collapsing with fatigue, exposure and hunger. They passed a second night on the ice, with Burns and Tours fading fast, until both died. Burns was a frail man for a sealer and died on the third day, with Tours on the fourth. Burns was not a common name in Banff, but there was a Burns family at 26 High Street, headed by a thirty-three year old widow. If this was the same family, it is likely that James was the eldest son, so his death would be doubly tragic for a mother already struggling.

The others struggled to survive. On the third day they sailed out in the captain's boat and captured seals, which they killed and brought back to be eaten raw. The remaining twenty-four men survived that night, and the next, their fourth on the ice with inadequate clothing and food. On the fifth day a group of volunteers again rowed out in the captain's boat to search for help, and this time their luck returned. They saw a sail to the south.

It is difficult to imagine the mixed feelings, of elation, hope and apprehension that this ship might also pass them by. Returning to the ice floe, they informed the others. At once Captain Hay organised that the fittest and strongest entered the boat and rowed to the distant ship.

The vessel proved to be *Brahmoor,* a Hanoverian sealer, which was now sailing to the whaling grounds in the north. The master immediately picked up the men who had rowed to him and lent Captain Hay a boat's crew of his own men to collect the remainder.

Even when on board *Brahmoor,* the effects of four days of bitter cold and lack of food took their toll. Not surprisingly, many men suffered from frostbite and Mr Allen, the mate, had to have his limbs amputated. He died shortly afterward. The men of *Brahmoor* looked after the crew of *Felix* until they could transfer them to other Scottish whaling vessels, which eventually brought them home. There was one final casualty, for when Mr Allen's wife heard about the death of her husband, she also passed away. There were always hidden casualties in any tragedy.

While the crew of *Felix* was suffering, the other Greenland vessels were battling what proved to be a very stormy season, and the sealing ships kept a look out for boats that had been driven astray from their parent vessel. Despite the weather, the second Banff vessel, *Alexander Harvey*, had captured around 2300 seals by the end of April, which was better than her total for the previous year but not enough to make a successful season. After the loss of one vessel, the people of Banff would wait anxiously for news of *Alexander Harvey*, but toward the end of June the Fraserburgh vessel *Vulcan* brought better news.

Vulcan reported that *Alexander Harvey* was safe and had had around 25 to 30 tuns of oil. There would have been mixed feelings when the wives heard she had gone onto the whaling grounds. Nevertheless, *Alexander Harvey* returned safely at the end of July, but without great success at the whaling. After the optimism and high hopes of the previous season, 1854 had been a bad year for Banff.

Nevertheless, even with the loss of *Felix*, Banff continued to progress as a port. According to the Aberdeen Tide Tables for 1856, the overall

Banff fleet had risen in the previous decade. In 1841 Banff had possessed 23 vessels with a total of 1800 tons, a figure that remained steady for a decade, but by 1856 there were 27 vessels with an aggregate tonnage of 2500. Despite the tragedy of *Felix*, the shipping future of Banff appeared secure.

There was less fanfare about the sealing in 1855, with *Alexander Harvey* as Banff's sole representative and no attempt to replace *Felix*. By the end of January preparations were advanced, and once again there was a farewell ball, this time held in the old hall of St Andrews Lodge. As in the previous year, the ball was a success, with the Earl of Fife, providing £2 and a large cake, while in return the revellers drunk his health. At the end of the evening there was a profit of £1, which was distributed to the local sailor's widows.

Alexander Harvey sailed on the 17th February, and no doubt the people of Banff watched her go, some thinking of the loss of *Felix*. They would wait with the usual mixture of fatalism and anxiety throughout the spring and summer months, and there would be joy on the 31st July when *Active* of Peterhead returned with news that *Alexander Harvey* had caught a whale. However that news was later proved false when she sailed in a week later with a cargo of just 800 seals. However, she did have two live polar bears, which were the objects of great interest and anecdotes that again proved the different attitudes of Victorians to nature.

The crew had been sealing north of latitude 73 when they saw a mother bear and her two cubs. Shooting the mother, they looped ropes over the heads of the two cubs and promptly dragged them back to the ship. Throwing each cub into a separate cask, the men kept them in place with an iron grating and treated them like pets for the remainder of the voyage. Eventually the male became so tame he could be fed by hand. The crew intended to give or sell the bears to a zoo, and during the voyage they also killed eleven other bears and brought home the skins and some of the heads and paws.

Despite the capture of two polar bear cubs, the relative failure of *Alexander Harvey* on that trip with only 800 seals, following upon the loss of *Felix* the previous year, marked the end of Banff's venture into the sealing trade. In September of that year the owners of the sealing firm sold *Alexander Harvey* to Charles McBeath of Fraserburgh and bowed gracefully out of what, two years previously, had seemed a very lucrative business. It was left to Fraserburgh to carry the mantle of the Moray Firth sealing and whaling trade.

Chapter Six

THE DANGERS OF THE NORTH

At 12pm stuck fast in the ice and backed astern but of no avail; called all hands to roll the ship which they did with a will
Matthew Campbell, Diary of a Voyage to the Davis Straits, 27 June 1884

Whaling and sealing, like any branch of sailoring, was a dangerous occupation. The journals of the surgeons and others are peppered with examples of people being injured, getting lost, being frostbitten or dying in the north in proportional numbers that perhaps only the armed forces or fishermen face today. Seamen from the Moray Firth were no safer than any others when they chose the sealing or whaling trade, but very few left written accounts that have survived. For that reason, many of the examples used here are culled from the pens of men who sailed from other ports, but although the particular incidents may not concern Moray Firth seamen, they shared exactly the same dangers.

Seafaring itself was a hazardous occupation, with ships running aground or worse, vanishing without trace. The statistics of the government's *Report of Shipwrecks* make hideous reading; for instance, in 1835 there were 524 British vessels stranded or wrecked, with a further 30 missing or lost. Of these, in nineteen instances, the entire crews were drowned so that year alone there were a known 564 seamen drowned at sea. In 1848, according to the Shipping Returns, there were 501 sailing vessels lost, with a further 25 steam powered vessels. There are no official figures for the number of seamen after 1835.

One reason for these shocking figures was the poor training of the master and officers. Until the middle of the nineteenth century, many masters, particularly of coastal craft, had little formal education and navigated by dead reckoning, which meant they estimated their position. Some neither used sextant nor charts, so it is hardly surprising that every storm littered the coasts of Scotland, Wales and England with broken ships and battered seamen.

There had been a tentative and very slow movement toward improving aspects of mercantile shipping since the end of the 18th century. In 1786 the General Registry Act had ordered that each British ship should have its origin recorded, along with its builder and owner, its tonnage and details of its size and rig. This act did nothing to alleviate the many hardships of the seamen, who were open to physical abuse by the officers at sea, were often cheated in port and could be drowned by ignorant officers who knew nothing of navigation.

In 1845 a voluntary scheme was created for examinations for masters and mates of foreign going vessels only, which was useless for the huge numbers of seamen who worked on the coastal craft. In 1854 the British Government improved on this when it passed the Merchant Shipping Act that tightened up regulations at sea. Only after that act were officers in merchant vessels ordered to show they were proficient navigators and ship handlers. That act also began a very slight improvement in the welfare of seamen by requiring that both masters and hands signed a record of the seaman's character, conduct and position on the ship.

By the 1854 Act, the master of every ship and the first and second mate of a foreign going ship, which included the Greenland vessels, had to have a certificate to prove their competency afloat, or had a number of years of service at sea. Any vessel of 100 tons or above had to have a certificated master and certificated mate. The second mate had to be at least seventeen years old, with four years sea experience and an understanding of the first five rules of arithmetic, the use of longitude and how to use a sextant. If there was only one mate, he had to be at least nineteen years old with five years sea experience and be able to navigate by the sun, while a first mate had to have sufficient knowledge to 'observe azimuths and compute the variation, compare chronometers and work the latitude by single altitude of the sun.'

With each increase the rank, the ship's officer had to have a correspondingly great knowledge of nautical matters, until finally the ship's master, who had to be at least twenty-one with six years seagoing experience and a thorough knowledge of seamanship and navigation. The Act also restricted the number of shares in a vessel to 64, and directed that all the owners should be recorded. This Act went some way to alleviating some of the abuses of ships sailing with incompetent or inexperienced officers, but there were still a plethora of dangers that lay just beyond the harbour mouth.

As with crewmen on any ship, whaling and sealing seamen faced the possibility of ordinary sickness, while the surgeon had to cope with the ordinary shipboard perils of colds and coughs, with broken bones or sprains and sundry cuts and bruises. In addition he had the worry of frostbite and, on longer voyages or if trapped in the ice, of scurvy. There may also have been venereal diseases. Writing on the 6th June 1856, Surgeon Trotter, on *Enterprise*, said "the worst perhaps I had was a case of lockjaw which...I soon cured, not, however before I had to bleed the man." He also mentioned a helmsman "knocked clean over the wheel" because "a piece of ice having struck the helm ... he was carried into the cabin insensible, his neck being nearly broken."

The weather was a constant threat, with gales frequent in the north. On the 10th July Trotter mentions this factor "a heavy gale of wind today with a tremendous sea sweeping over the decks." Sometimes the gale would take a seaman or two, and on a dark night their loss might not even missed until any possibility of rescue was gone. The laconic entry in the journal of Surgeon Matthew Campbell of the Dundee *Nova*

Zembla on 21 March 1884 says it all: "two men missing from the mate's watch. Must have been washed overboard."

At other times the danger was less immediate but more widespread. Ships needed to keep their stores up to scratch, for even drinking water might run out, or turn foul, over time. As John Wanless, surgeon of the Dundee vessel *Thomas* said on the 16 May 1834, "The longer we live the more unfortunate are we. The fresh water has an odious taste among our other miseries that we cannot receive a good drink of water." Fortunately there was usually a handy remedy for this particular hardship. Here is Campbell again, on the 6th May 1884: "we got nearly a tank of water off a small berg in the afternoon, we being in great need of water."

Sometimes the entire ship would go down, such as *Empress of India* in 1859. Nearby vessels steamed to the scene, but not always with the best of intentions. This short piece is from the journal of Thomas Macklin of *Narwhal*: "tried to save as much as possible from the wreck ... together with the crew of the *Empress* and our men – both, I am ashamed to say, showering the most obscene oaths upon each other." On that occasion the crew of *Narwhal* and the Norwegian members of *Empress of India* were nearly out of hand, fighting each other and searching for the spirit locker and only the intervention of *Narwhal's* master and officers prevented what could have become a very nasty riot.

It was a tradition among whaling men that when the ship founded, they made free with the rum, and the loss of *Empress* was no different. Macklin wrote: "In the cabin the scene was one of great confusion. Captain Martin was armed to the teeth and his duty required great firmness ... the whole of the men were pressing down demanding rum." Such behaviour seems to have been fairly acceptable after a wreck, for William Barron mentioned, in page 22 of his book Old Whaling Days that when a ship was wrecked the hands "tumbled the rum puncheon out of the cabin. The head was knocked out of the cask and tins and boots were dipped in the rum." Barron believed that many were permanently injured by their drunkenness, and added "the following morning somebody set the wreck on fire." Similar scenes were recorded during the Baffin Fair of 1830, when half the British whaling fleet was caught in the ice; nineteen vessels were wrecked and upward of a thousand men caroused around the looted rum casks.

Sometimes the dangers were more subtle than simple shipwreck and mayhem. The early whaling vessels carried the blubber in casks and in 1802 Captain Alexander Young of the Montrose vessel *Eliza Swan* reported to the Customs Officers that when the crew were filling the casks with blubber, "eleven of the people … nearly lost their lives in the hold by Mephitic Air which issued from a number of water casks which were stashed for the purpose of being filled with blubber."

Whaling then, was a dangerous occupation. As well as the normal hazards of the sea there were the extra perils of icebergs, frostbite and being trapped for an unknown length of time in sub-zero conditions. It was no disgrace that the Banff Sealing and Whaling Company had failed to make a profit, but another Moray Firth port, Fraserburgh, was also active in the Arctic.

Chapter Seven

THE FRASERBURGH SEALING AND WHALING TRADE: THE 1850s

> *The seasonal nature and short voyages of Scottish whalers attracted a class of seamen who, living in the ships home port, sailed in them year after year. This made for a happier atmosphere aboard them'*
> Captain G. W. Clark: The Last of the Whaling Captains

Situated right on the knuckle of the great fist of Buchan that punches out into the North Sea, Fraserburgh had to be a nautical town. With Kinnaird Head as an outlier and Fraserburgh Bay curving to the east, the town enjoys a spectacular situation. Fraserburgh has long had a rivalry with Peterhead, a few miles further south, and in the 19th century both were involved in the sealing and whaling trade. The history of Fraserburgh is long and interesting.

Known to the locals as the Broch, which is the old Scots term for a burgh, its original 14th century name was Faithlie but in the early 16th century Fraser of Philorth bought the town and began to recreate it in the image of his family. At first the alterations and improvements were gradual, with the construction of a harbour in 1546, and a castle on Kinnaird Head thirty years later. In 1592 Faithlie became Fraserburgh, and the town also became a burgh of regality. Sir Alexander Fraser of Philorth was elevated, becoming Lord Saltoun, a name that was later to resound within the sealing industry. The Frasers were ambitious landlords and attempted to found a university here, but while that scheme failed, the fishing industry did not.

In 1787 the two hundred year old castle became a lighthouse and a few decades later Scotland's first mainland lighthouse station was established. It was obvious that the sea was vital for the future. In the late eighteenth and for much of the nineteenth centuries, fishing was a Scottish boom industry. Fraserburgh expanded, taking over the neighbouring village of Broadsea and enlarging the harbour in long phases of improvement. In 1810 herring curing started in Fraserburgh and the enlarged harbour was eventually able to hold the hundreds of fishing boats that crowded in. Nevertheless, there were also envious eyes directed at nearby Peterhead, whose whaling and sealing fleet was the largest in Britain and in the early 1850s, Fraserburgh joined in the sealing boom.

Although the town was never to rival Peterhead, for a while Fraserburgh was an important sealing and whaling port. At its peak, it sent six vessels north, which meant that a considerable proportion of the Broch's manhood were involved in the Arctic, and although the number of vessels quickly diminished, Fraserburgh retained an interest in whaling and sealing for the best part of twenty years. As with every whaling port, Fraserburgh would be polluted from time to time with the smell of boiling whale blubber when the ships were in. The boiling yards were on the links and a south easterly wind spread the appalling smell over the town.

But what sort of people were these men who willingly put themselves in danger to hunt seals and whales amidst the ice of the Arctic? Ultimately, they were the ancestors of today's Scots; part of us. Any Scot can claim, in the words of Alexander Gray, that they were 'flesh of my flesh, and bone of my bone;' their actions helped create the fabric of Scotland, but although attached by blood, a waste of time and experience divides us.

It is almost impossible to delve into the minds and motives of people who lived in the past, for we are conditioned by our own environment and a culture that has undergone massive alterations since the high Victorian days of the 1850s and 1860s. The best we can do is read letters, journals and newspaper reports; sing their songs and visit museums to inspect the artefacts that are now curiosities but then were the essential realities of everyday life.

It is possible to tell a lot from the songs that people sing. Not the taught, cultured songs learned in places of education, but the ordinary, off-the-cuff choruses roared out while in the company of family or peers, people with whom the singer feels comfortable. Unfortunately again, many, probably most of such impromptu folk songs have been lost, or altered so completely by prim academics that the original words and feelings have been lost. What is left is a sanitised shell of reality, but perhaps some of the spirit survives in the verses of whaling songs such as *Farewell Tae Tarwathie*, written around the time of the Fraserburgh sealing trade by a New Deer miller named George Scroggie.

> *Farewell tae Tarwathie, adieu Mormond Hill*
> *And the dear land o' Crimond I bid ye farewell,*
> *I'm bound out for Greenland and ready to sail*
> *In hopes to find riches in hunting the whale.'*

However much sanitised *Tarwathie* may be, it does provide some clues of the feelings and motives of the mid-Victorian seal hunters. The sadness at parting and romanticised love of home, which is surely universal before any perilous voyage was tinged with excitement in the words 'I'm bound out for Greenland and ready to sail.' The word 'ready' suggests more than just a state of preparedness, but also a pent-up eagerness, a desire to be off, while the last line, 'hopes to find riches' gives the true motive. The Greenlandmen were not hunting purely for the lust of killing, but for money. Ultimately, seal or whale hunting provided a means of living.

Farewell to Tarwathie is still sung today in folk clubs up and down the country, as is *Bonny Ship the Diamond*, about the Peterhead whaling trade.

'Along the quay at Peterhead the lassies stand around
Wi their shawls all pulled about them and the saut tears runnin' doon.'

Once again there is the sorrow at parting, and the feeling of desolation in 'their shawls all pulled about them.' We have a picture of women weeping, huddled together in sorrow and against the raw cold of a February morning as the whaling fleet leaves for the north. It is a vision of sadness at the beginning of the voyage, and a complete contrast to the final line of relief, triumph and celebration.

These songs, and many more, were gathered by a collector of folk songs named Gavin Greig, a Buchan man himself who actively sought whaling material. Unfortunately for posterity, he deliberately did not record the more bawdy choruses that the Greenlandmen undoubtedly roared out, saying they were 'rather strong for print.' There is just a hint of such content in the last couplet of *Bonnie Ship the Diamond*:

We'll make the cradles for to rock and the blankets for to tear
And every lass in Peterhead sing 'Hushabye my dear

Although the Greenland vessels sailed from Banff and Fraserburgh, the crews would also come from the fishing villages along the coast of Buchan, Banffshire and Moray. To many fishermen, such as James Sim from Broadsea, whaling was a temporary occupation, something to be followed for a year or two to make enough money to invest in a fishing boat or a wife.

The names of many whaling men are recorded in log books and crew lists, but details of most are long gone. However, sometimes scraps remain. One of the best known women on this stretch of the Moray Firth coast was Christian Watt, who left an impressive journal that recorded her life of tragedy and sorrow, mingled with solid sense and an unquenchable aura of pride. In common with so many people along the Moray Firth coast, Christian Watt had an intimate connection with the sea. Her mother taught her that the seafarers in her family were superior to landsmen as they could "navigate small boats by oar, and sail to the Hebrides, Shetland and Greenland with nothing but the sextant set with the noonday sun, and the stars to guide them at night."

So even as a child, Christian knew of the Greenland connection, and the people of Broadsea, then separate from Fraserburgh, had whaling as part of their heritage. Broadsea was very much a maritime village, known as the Seatown in the old Fraserburgh Barony court books. Like so many Scottish fishing villages, it was very close knit, with strong family ties, and the Watts had lived in the same house for over two hundred years. The houses were small and simple, built in the vernacular style common to many Scottish villages. Some still had a central fire and recent memories of sharing with animals, but whatever their faults, they sheltered generations of hard working and intelligent people.

"My father" wrote Christian Watt in page 15 of her *Papers* "went to Greenland to the whaling, a very dangerous job costing many young lives. The whalers were a wild rough lot who lived for the day, never a year passed that some did not return."

There was no doubt that she was correct. Whaling, and the associated sealing, was a dangerous occupation. Her description of the whalers as a 'wild rough lot' tallies with other accounts that tell of Greenlandmen fighting among themselves or causing trouble when ashore. However it is hard to say if they were worse than any other British seamen, or indeed fishermen, who were also known to cause trouble when loose en-masse in Fraserburgh. Perhaps it would be fair to say that any large group of men, freed after a long stressful voyage, could become wild, particularly when combined with alcohol. On page 16, Watt also mentioned the stress endured by the families of the whaling men. "During the season it was trying time for those at home, for there was no communication with Greenland." Knowledge of this coming period would account for the "saut tears" in the first line of *Bonnie Ship the Diamond*.

That lack of communication is sometimes hard to understand in the 21st century, when technology brings people in instant contact with friends and family at the touch of a mobile phone button. The knowledge of months of simply not knowing what was happening to a son, brother or husband, even not being aware if they were alive or dead, or how many days, weeks or months they could be absent, must have increased the strain tremendously.

As well as her father, Christian Watt had a husband with whaling connections. In 1858 Christian and James Sim signed a bond of handfast, which was a very practical arrangement like a trial marriage that safeguarded any children but allowed for legal separation if the couple decided they were not right for a permanent union.

After a season at the Greenland whaling, and with Christian pregnant, James returned home in November and they married a few days later. Due to the strong will of his wife, James Sim soon returned to the fishing, and Christian's whaling connections ended. However, if she was typical of many fishwives of the Moray Firth coast, the connection between fishing and whaling was very strong, and the quality of whaling men on the Moray vessels very high.

It was such men who filled the Greenland ships that were to leave Fraserburgh for the best part of two decades. What follows is a season by season account of Fraserburgh's experience with the Arctic sealing and whaling trade.

1852 season

On the 21st February 1852 the 297-ton barque *Melinka* slipped out of Fraserburgh harbour, bound for the sealing grounds of the north. Captain John Stephen was in command. Captain John Stephen was one of a nautical family in Fraserburgh, with his brothers Peter and Alexander also being shipmasters, as was his father, John. He had previously been master of *Sir William Wallace*, sailing to London. Bought new at Belfast, *Melinka* was fitted out for both sealing and whaling. The people of the Broch, in particular her owners and the family of her crew, would watch her with a mixture of excitement and trepidation, for they knew of the profits and dangers of the Arctic trade.

The Greenlandmen would see the crowds of well wishers waving to them from the quays and the Castle Green, and then gradually the Broch would diminish astern, as would the final farewell from the lighthouse on Kinnaird Head; their thoughts would ease from their families and turn north, to the bitter Arctic and the sealing grounds.

As usual with whaling ships when heading out, *Melinka* was in ballast; the first of the Fraserburgh sealers, and she heralded an industry that was to last for nearly two decades. On that first voyage, *Melinka* was highly successful, and there are perhaps apocryphal tales of the crew throwing stores over the side to make room for more blubber. It could hardly be a more auspicious start to Fraserburgh's adventure with the north.

The people of the Broch again filled the Castle Green, cheering when *Melinka* returned undamaged to Fraserburgh Bay in the morning of the 18th May, the first ship to return from the seal fishing and with nearly 140 tuns of oil on board. Fraserburgh was abuzz with excitement at the news. As well as her satisfactorily full hold, *Melinka* carried news of other sealing and whaling vessels, none of which had exceeded her success, which must have caused her investors to purr with fulfilment.

Melinka had made her successful voyage despite some wild weather; she had left the ice on the 29th April, and made a quick passage home. All in all, Captain John Stephen should have been a happy man, and he would have been happier still when the Fraserburgh Whale and Seal Fishing Company, *Melinka*'s owners put aside 3% of profit for further investment and still declared a 43% dividend for the shareholders. This company bought a further ship, *Vulcan* and had her strengthened for the ice, while a rival company worked on *Sovereign*. The sealing industry was thriving in Fraserburgh. *Vulcan* was another tough little ship, originally built for the iron trade and had been bought from the Carron Iron Company.

The success of *Melinka* encouraged others in Fraserburgh to invest money in the sealing industry and there was a sudden rush of people who discovered a common interest in the north. Speculation was mooted of two further vessels leaving Fraserburgh the following season. The same company that owned *Melinka*, it was said, would send out a 265-ton barque *Elim* that was partly owned by the local businessman Charles McBeath, while Messrs Park and Wemyss would fit out *Anna Mary*, another barque of 303 tons. Although these ships never sailed north, the first season closed on a satisfactory buzz of financial and professional pride.

1853 season

In the event, the Fraserburgh fleet did indeed increase the following season. The first ship to leave the Broch was *Melinka*, the next was the 177 ton brig *Vulcan* under Captain Alexander in late February with the 130 ton brig *Sovereign*, commanded by Captain Burnett following on the 23rd. *Sovereign* and *Vulcan* were older and smaller vessels and were intended only for the sealing rather than the more vigorous work at whaling. Fraserburgh had invested a great deal of money in these vessels, with £7000 on *Melinka* alone, £3000 on *Vulcan* and £2,600 on *Sovereign*. The shareholders expected a good return for their money. James Cardno managed *Sovereign*.

That month was stormy, with a number of wrecks along the north east coasts of Scotland. There was consternation when the sea washed up a shattered whaleboat at Port Gordon, near Buckie. Local fishermen read the inscribed name *Melinka*, and feared the worst, particularly as a ship's foremast was also cast ashore. However, by the 15th all three Fraserburgh vessels had reached Lerwick, despite further fears that *Vulcan* had foundered en-route and by the time the vessels left for the fishing, there were 125 whaling men on board.

Like *Melinka* the previous season, *Sovereign* returned rapidly from the sealing, arriving in Fraserburgh Bay in early May. As would be expected, the town was lively and crowds gathered at the quays and around the lighthouse.

There was no need for anxiety. Captain Burnett's *Sovereign* had returned because she had captured a sizeable number of seals and her holds were full with 35 tons of oil and the skins of 3000seals. *Melinka* came home soon after with 8000 seals and 95 tons of oil, while Captain

Alexander's *Vulcan* brought back 3000 skins and 40 tons of oil. The sealing was successful, for next season, all three vessels again sailed north.

1854 Season

Two of the ships, *Vulcan* under Captain Alexander, and *Melinka* under Captain John Stephen left on the 13th February, sailing into the same series of gales that had troubled the Banff vessels and which blew some of the Peterhead vessels as far south as the Forth. *Sovereign* left slightly later, while *Lady Campbell*, the solitary Nairn sealer, left Aberdeen, ran straight into trouble and on the 27th February put into Fraserburgh for repairs.

That was a stormy year at the sealing, with heavy ice that smashed some of the whaleboats and damaged the mother ships. *Felix* of Banff was lost. The three Fraserburgh ships, however, survived the gales to return safely, and with a decent enough catch to ensure a profit for the shareholders. By t*he 27th April Melinka had* caught 3000 seals, with *Sovereign* having 1000 and Vulcan 2000. *Sovereign* under Captain Barnett was first to arrive on the 23rd May. By then she had captured 2500 seals; she had a difficult voyage, losing two boats and being damaged by the ice. The other Fraserburgh ships straggled in over the next few days. The loss of *Felix* must have had a sobering effect on the Moray Firth ports, but there was no hint of the merchants from Fraserburgh giving up on the new industry. The sealing ships spent the winter being refitted and readied for the next season while the crews would either work elsewhere or live off their wages and oil money.

In 1854 the oil merchants T & C Lawrence of Peterhead published a list showing the number and tonnage of ships in the British sealing and whaling fleets. The greatest number came from Peterhead, which had 28 vessels from a total British figure of 51. The Moray Firth ports provided 6 vessels, over 10% of the total, with Fraserburgh's three vessels the fourth highest equal, behind Hull and Dundee. It was not a bad position to be in for a port that had only been in the trade for three years.

1855 Season

By February 1855, the Fraserburgh sealing fleet was again ready to face the ice. On the 17th February *Melinka* and *Vulcan* left harbour with *Sovereign* sailing a few days later. Their plan was for all three vessels to try the Greenland seal fishing first, but if *Melinka* did not catch her quota, she could round Cape Farewell at the southern tip of Greenland and go to the Davis Strait whaling. There was also an option for *Melinka* to over winter in the ice, following the trail blazed by other Scottish vessels. In the event *Melinka* had no need to remain in the ice and she returned home with a more than decent catch.

As in every whaling and sealing port, Fraserburgh experienced her share of minor tragedies. For example a 26 year old boatsteerer seaman named Alexander William Geddes fell overboard from a returning vessel and drowned, only 20 miles from home. Although the family would mourn, the owners would be more concerned with profit and the incident was barely mentioned.

With their vessels consistently making them a profit, the Fraserburgh merchants increased their speculation and in July 1855 they bought another vessel, *Enterprise*, from her Peterhead owners. James Cardno managed this vessel. With four vessels, the Fraserburgh fleet was now the equal third largest in terms of British sealing. Built in Stockport in 1844, *Enterprise* was a 397-ton barque, which made her the largest vessel to sail from Fraserburgh at that time. She carried a crew of sixty, not including the invaluable addition of the Shetland men. A tall vessel, *Enterprise* had masts that soared eighty feet toward the grey Arctic sky, so she would be a striking ship when she entered Fraserburgh Bay. No sooner had *Enterprise* made the short journey around the knuckle of Buchan to settle in her new harbour, than Fraserburgh extended itself again and bought a fifth vessel.

Banff never seemed to quite recover its confidence after the loss of *Felix*, so it may have been no surprise when Charles McBeath of Fraserburgh bought the second Banff Greenland vessel, *Alexander Harvey*. Charles McBeath was a Fraserburgh born shipowner and fish curer. According to the 1851 census, he would be 37 in 1852, married to Eliza and with three daughters and one son. At that time he lived at 98 School Street, only a few houses along from Mr Milne the harbourmaster at number 102.

By purchasing this ship, Fraserburgh became the third largest whaling centre in Britain, and the *Banffshire Journal* echoed the glow of pride felt by the town. The Fraserburgh correspondent stated "we have great pleasure (in congratulating) ourselves on the success ... and the spirit of energy and enterprise which our townsmen have shown themselves to possess." Although this slightly bombastic view is typically Victorian, it was also true: Fraserburgh had done splendidly to increase its sealing fleet from one ship to five within four years, while other, much longer established ports, languished on two or three vessels. There is also no doubting the fact that Fraserburgh had increased the weight of its shipping by 1000 tons that year alone. The future looked bright for the Broch.

It was the beginning of October before *Alexander Harvey* arrived in Fraserburgh, arriving in the harbour with a rising tide slightly after midnight. A new company with Charles McBeath and Mr George Wallace, agent of the Union Bank as joint managers was set up to own her, and gave command to John Stephen's brother, Captain Alexander Stephen, late of *Vigilant*. Such was the interest in the sealing company that the shares were nearly all snapped up even before the ship arrived in harbour. Charles McBeath was an important man in Fraserburgh, for as well as being involved in the sealing industry, he was unanimously re-elected as a harbour commissioner, along with Thomas Walker. As a merchant and shipowner, he was also on the provisional committee for the Aberdeen, Peterhead and Fraserburgh Railway, along with Thomas Walker, so McBeath was moving constantly in the highest circles. Fraserburgh sealing was obviously considered a trade for the elite.

The sealing fleet had provided a boost for Fraserburgh shipping, but the port had expanded its overall tonnage greatly during the previous fourteen years. In 1840 there had been fourteen vessels belonging to Fraserburgh, with a total tonnage of 1419. By the end of 1855 there were 34 vessels, and a tonnage of 5996. Of the total, the Greenland fleet made up five vessels and 1219 tons, about one seventh the number of vessels, but one fifth of the weight. In 1855 seal oil had sold for £12,635, which was a large sum of money for the time, so justifying the investment of the ship owners and shareholders.

The Aberdeen Tide Tables confirm the trend in Fraserburgh shipping, with figures of 14 vessels and 1392 tons in 1841, 22 ships and 2360 tons in 1856 and 30 ships and 3178 tons in 1851, even before the sealing fleet came about. Presumably this constant increase in shipping had helped create the wealth that was available to be invested in the Greenland vessels.

To further heighten enthusiasm in the sealing trade, and to prove that success had rewards other than itself, in September 1855 the Fraserburgh Seal and Whale Fishing Company presented Captain John Stephen of *Melinka* with a gold watch and chain as a token of their appreciation for his zeal. Captain John Stephen deserved his award, for under his command *Melinka* had brought home over 400 tuns of seal oil.

Despite the undoubted success of the sealing trade, the advent of these new large vessels caused problems for Fraserburgh harbour. In common with many Scottish harbours, Fraserburgh was in constant need of improvement and enlargement throughout the nineteenth century as vessels became ever larger.

1856 season

For the 1856 season, the larger vessels of the now five strong Fraserburgh fleet were ready for their voyage north by the beginning of February, some weeks earlier than was strictly necessary. That was because the deep draughted vessels needed a high spring tide to leave harbour and they were always apprehensive that a sudden storm might delay them until the next, much later spring tide. Mr McBeath and his colleagues were unhappy at this early start, however necessary, because they had to pay and feed the crew for a longer period. There were harbour improvements in progress, however, which would eventually ease matters for the larger vessels.

The difficulties did not end there, for with the sealing vessels sitting in harbour for long periods of time, other vessels were more crowded, and it seemed that the trade had reached its maximum extent. Unless the harbour was enlarged, there could be no more additions to the Fraserburgh fleet. So for all its ambitions for the future, Fraserburgh could not compete with Peterhead without enlarging and deepening the present harbour. The merchants had to balance the expenditure involved with improvements with the possibility of further profit from the Greenland fleet, and other merchant adventures.

The three largest Fraserburgh vessels left on the most convenient tide early in February 1856, with the much smaller *Vulcan*, under Captain Noble, and *Sovereign*, commanded by Captain Samuel, sailing a week later. In a stormy passage north, *Vulcan* lost her fore topmast and topgallant mast even before she reached Shetland, but such things were the usual hazards of the sea and she was repaired and continued with the sealing.

Once again, the last vessels out were the first to return, with *Vulcan* returning in mid June, carrying only 1500 seals. However, most of them were the larger old seals that yielded more oil, so the cargo was estimated at between 20 and 25 tuns. On arrival, her master reported that *Melinka*, *Enterprise* and *Alexander Harvey* had all sailed for the whaling, but he did not know if they had been successful at the sealing. He did think, however, that *Sovereign* had '8 or 9' tuns of seal oil. When Captain Grey brought *Active* back into Peterhead he reported that *Enterprise* had 1000 seals and one whale with a total of 15 tuns of oil, while Captain Stephen of *Melinka* had 2000 seals and four whales, with 40 tuns of oil. The shareholders and people of Fraserburgh had to wait to see if the report was accurate.

Captain John Stephen of *Melinka* was the last to return, but with all the vessels accounted for, the final total for the 1856 season was verified. Captain Alexander Stephen of *Alexander Harvey* proved the most successful ship with 3000 seals and four whales, yielding a total of 60 tuns of oil, with *Melinka* second on 1800 seals and 40 tuns. The third vessel home was the much smaller *Vulcan*, with 1200 seals but no whales, and then a disappointing 900 seals but one whale from the larger *Enterprise*. Expectedly last was the smallest vessel, *Sovereign* with 700 seals and 7 tons of oil.

As usual, the figures did not correspond exactly with others. T & Lawrence, the Peterhead oil merchants, compiled their own tables, which gave *Alexander Harvey* 3067 seals and 40 tons of seal oil, with *Melinka* at 1814 and 13 tuns, *Vulcan* at 1423 and 18 tuns, *Enterprise* at 900 and 10 tuns and *Sovereign* at 690 and 7 tuns. That same source stated that the total value of the seal and whale fishings for 1856 was £198, 684, with Peterhead having £77,560 and Fraserburgh a respectable £7,727. Both ports, however, experienced a considerable drop in revenue from the previous year.

Despite the totals not being as high as hoped for, the very scarcity of catches pushed up prices, so that the shareholders would not be too disappointed. That season seal oil was selling at up to £49 a tun in Peterhead and sealskins in Fraserburgh were fetching from 4/7d (23p) to 4/11 (24.5p) a skin, and the prices seemed to be rising. There seemed to be a dearth of oil casks in Fraserburgh that season, for a ship arrived from Dundee carrying a cargo of them, which implies a connection between the Dundee and Fraserburgh seal industry. A second connection came later that year when two vessels, *John Duncan* of Dundee and *Stephen* of Fraserburgh, carried cargos of seal oil south to Dundee. Given that Dundee had been involved in the whaling and sealing trade since 1752, importing oil from such a newcomer as Fraserburgh surely indicated a failure in their own trade, or rising demand in the city. However, the merchants of Dundee would soon put their industry to rights.

There was a break from tradition in August that year when Captain Stephen took *Melinka* around the north coast of Scotland in search of whales. She called in at Wick at a time that a shoal of up to thirty whales were seen in the Pentland Firth.

In the meantime, Fraserburgh made hay while the oil sun shined. In September 1856 the shareholders of the Fraserburgh Whale and Seal Fishing Company had a cheerful meeting in the Commissioners Hall and decided to double the capital of the company to £20,000. The owners of *Alexander Harvey*, the most successful of the 1856 fleet, were even more pleased as they received a 20% dividend. The Fraserburgh seal fishing industry seemed to be going from strength to strength.

1857 season

Once again, in 1857 the Fraserburgh vessels sailed at different dates, with the three larger vessels sailing around the 10th of February and the two smaller a week later. Again the larger vessels were fitted for seal and whale fishing, while the smaller were for seal fishing only. Around the same time the Fraserburgh Harbour Bill was referred to the Select Committee on Standing Orders. This bill was designed to improve the harbour, partly for the convenience of the sealing fleet. That bill stammered on, with an initial proposal under a former act to borrow £20,000 being doubled to £40,000.

If the 1856 season was slightly disappointing, that of 1857 was worse. The first portent of future disaster was not even recognised as such when *Jackall,* an 8-ton steam driven screw propeller craft arrived at Peterhead from the Clyde. With a 20 horsepower engine and rigged as a fore and aft schooner, she was intended to accompany the whaler *Traveller* to the fishing grounds. There was also a steam whaler waiting in the Clyde for Captain Sutter of Peterhead to return from the sealing so he could take her to the whale fishing. With all the vessels of Fraserburgh, as well as Peterhead being purely sail powered, any success by a steamer would have put their future in jeopardy. The Fraserburgh fleet would be instantly outdated, and the company shareholders would have the choice of battling on with old-fashioned technology, or investing heavily in new vessels. However, at that stage the future was unclear, the steam vessels untested and the future still seemed bright.

Nevertheless, results from the 1857 season were very disappointing as reports stuttered in from returning vessels. Captain Bruce of the Peterhead vessel *Resolution*, calling at Lerwick reported that *Melinka* had only 700 seals, while *Sovereign* and *Vulcan* had managed to capture only 300 apiece. Even worse, Bruce believed that the unfortunate *Enterprise* was clean: she had caught nothing at all. After their financial exertions in raising more capital, the Fraserburgh merchants must have wondered if it was all worthwhile.

The first of the Fraserburgh vessels to return was Captain Samuel's *Sovereign* with 1332 seals, which was a fair catch, made better by the fact that many were old, larger seals. In total *Sovereign* was expected to have 20 tuns of oil. She reported that *Melinka* had an impressive 110 tuns of oil, with *Alexander Harvey* 40 tuns and *Vulcan* between 30 and 40. The perennially unfortunate *Enterprise* however, was struggling with only about 12 to 14 tuns, but, together with *Alexander Harvey*, had sailed north to try the whaling. *Vulcan*, equipped only for sealing, returned on the 15th June with a more than respectable 45 tuns of oil.

Reports of the Fraserburgh vessels continued to arrive; with Captain Martin of the Peterhead vessel *Intrepid* claiming that *Alexander Harvey* had 1800 seals, 32 tuns of oil but no whales. On the 3rd August *Enterprise* returned with only 14 tuns of oil and not a single whale, and five days later *Alexander Harvey* arrived with 35 tuns of oil and a single whale, which was expected to yield another 9 or 10 tuns of oil. Although, with the exception of *Melinka*, the fishing had not been spectacular, the Fraserburgh vessels had been more successful than most other ports, so once again, despite their earlier scare, the company shareholders had little reason to grumble.

Lawrence of Peterhead again made a very useful list of catches from the various ports, and this shows that the Fraserburgh vessels held up well against the others. While Peterhead, with 31 vessels, caught 74,337 seals, the five Fraserburgh vessels accounted for 15,245, or an average of around 3,082 per vessel compared to around 2,038 from Peterhead. In whaling, however, Fraserburgh showed poorly. In the total value of the catch, Fraserburgh performed very well indeed. While the overall British total fell to £125,103, Fraserburgh increased its total by around £5,000. Despite some bad results, the seal fishing continued to show promise.

That year seal oil sold for £43 a tun, with one parcel of 'naked' oil, or oil that was not held within a cask, sold at £44 10/- a tun, but the market for skins had fallen through. Whale bone was at a premium, possibly because of the rise in popularity of the crinoline, which was beginning to dominate the female fashion market, and bone could make £200 a ton. There was even one figure of £510 a ton mentioned. Once again Fraserburgh exported her seal oil to other ports, with Newcastle and Aberdeen buying it that winter.

1858 season

By 1858 there were more changes to the whaling industry. Steam powered vessels were making an appearance in some ports, and the method of harpooning was also being modernised. Until now most vessels had hunted whales with hand harpoons, when the mother ship sent out small boats with a group of oarsmen headed by a harpooner, line manager and boatsteerer. While the oarsmen did the rowing, the boatsteerer steered by using a long oar, the linemanager made sure that the line, once attached to the whale by a harpoon, did not kink around anybody's leg and thus put him in danger of being dragged overboard if the whale should give a sudden spurt. Next to the shipmaster, the harpooner was arguably the most important man on board, for it was his responsibility to actually thrust the harpoon into the whale.

However, by the end of the 1850s, the method of hunting the whales was virtually obsolete. Rather than have a harpooner balancing in the bow of the boat as it was rowed forward across often choppy and icy seas, there would be a harpoon gun sitting in the bow, so all the harpooner had to do was point and click. By pulling the trigger, the harpooner would send a harpoon into the whale, or at least in its general direction. It may have been less romantic and probably less skilful, but it was also less dangerous. Although there had been attempts to invent an efficient whale-catching harpoon gun, not until 1792 was the problem taken seriously when the Society of Arts volunteered a prize for a successful weapon. Many tried, but nobody really created a harpoon gun that was any more efficient than a man with a steady hand and iron nerve. The gentle art of whale killing remained largely un-mechanised until the middle of the 19th century.

In 1858 *Melinka* and *Alexander Harvey* were fitted with the harpoon guns, which the Fraserburgh artisan Robert Tindall manufactured, so the whale ships were supporting a local industry. The guns had been successfully tested in the harbour and bay at Fraserburgh before they were approved as suitable for the Arctic.

This year the three largest vessels were due out around the 17th February, with the others following later. *Enterprise* was first to leave, and *Vulcan* and *Sovereign* last, but this time they sailed direct for the sealing grounds without picking up extra hands at Shetland. Once again they sailed into severe weather, which was not unexpected in the north, and once again the women of Fraserburgh waited to hear news of their men.

As the whalers and sealers battled the northern storms, Lord Saltoun, Fraser of Philorth, returned to his roots. On the 22 March the Fraserburgh schooner *Glengrant* sailed to Inverness to pick up His Lordship's furniture from his alternative home at Ness Castle and bring it to Philorth House just outside Fraserburgh. The contrast with the living conditions and style of the sealing men could hardly have been greater.

As always, news of the sealing fleet trickled from returning vessels. *Alibi* of Aberdeen reported having seen *Alexander Harvey*, and said that *Enterprise* had captured 1000 seals, while *Melinka* had been seen on the 23 April with another impressive catch of 3000 seals. *Vulcan* was reported to have 200, but *Sovereign* was clean. Three weeks later *Eliza* of Peterhead had reported that *Alexander Harvey* had only 200 seals and *Enterprise* carried 10 tuns of oil, while *Melinka*, never a ship to be beaten, had 5000 seals, with *Vulcan* carrying 35 tuns and

Sovereign 22 tuns. So all the Fraserburgh ships were safe, and all were catching seals.

By the middle of June the ships were beginning to drift back to Fraserburgh. On the 14th *Enterprise* and *Sovereign* returned, with *Vulcan* a day later. *Melinka* arrived on the 1st of August, with *Alexander Harvey* following the next day. Both ships had been reasonably successful at the seal fishing but, despite Mr Tindall's patent harpoon guns, neither had caught a whale. As usual, *Melinka* was the more successful vessel, with 70 tuns of oil compared to *Alexander Harvey's* 20, but that triumph was muted by the loss of one of her men. Joseph Noble, a Fraserburgh seaman on *Melinka*, had died of consumption (tuberculosis) on the voyage and the returning ship carried his remains.

Despite their outdoor lifestyle, lung diseases were fairly common amongst seamen, possibly because of the cramped living conditions within the forecastle where they spent their off-duty hours. As another example, here is an entry from the Leith whaler *North Pole* in 1837: "William Cownfoot Apprentice Departed the ship at the Surgeon Request for inflammation of the lungs." John Wanless, surgeon of the Dundee whaler *Thomas* in 1834 also mentioned a death on board *North Pole* when it was necessary '"to commit to the deep the last remains of a seaman who died of consumption."

There is no doubt that British seamen, who worked in some savage conditions and created much of the wealth of the country, were ill-considered when it came to comfortable, or even reasonable, living accommodation. They were a hardy breed but were expected to survive in tiny cabins that would have disgraced a prison.

Even with the Greenland ships safe back in harbour, things were not peaceful in Fraserburgh. Autumn is often a stormy time along the Moray Firth coast, and that autumn of 1858 was no exception. The storm of the 7th October screamed against the coast and drove ships ashore in a welter of ripping canvas and splintered spars.

The gale rose out of nothing, for the morning had been quiet, with a very slight southerly wind but soon after noon the North West wind increased, together with a heavy swell that thundered surf along the bay of Fraserburgh and rain that drove against people, buildings and vessels. By three in the afternoon the gale had risen to a storm, driving *Isabella Forbes* of Aberdeen into the bay with her cargo of Icelandic ponies and throwing *James Trail* of Thurso and *Fox* of Wick ashore. More significantly was the loss of the Prussian schooner *Fortuna* of Griefswald, with Captain Busan in command as she headed for Holyhead with railway sleepers. Coming into Fraserburgh Bay, the wind drove her on to the sand between Fraserburgh and Cairnbulg Head at four on Friday morning the 8th of October.

The Fraserburgh coastguard, headed by Mr Beatson immediately rushed to help, fired his mortar to secure a line on board and brought all the crew and even some of their possessions on shore by seven in the morning. Fortunately, *Fortuna* herself was only slightly damaged.

Within a few weeks a local merchant, Mr Oliphant, bought *Fortuna* and brought her into the harbour. She was found to be in reasonable repair and was taken on to the slip for repair, where although she was not heavily built, it was decided to adapt her as another sealing vessel. At 180 tons she would be larger than *Vulcan* or *Sovereign*. The men who effected the rescue were not neglected, with the Board of Trade awarding S. Gorm, the chief boatman and his boatmen Malcolm Fleacher, John Goodridge and john Cormack £1 each, while the pilots William Stephen, William Noble and Andrew Noble received 10/- (50p). Mr Beatson, commanding the Fraserburgh Coastguard was given the thanks of the Committee of the Privy Council for Trade and the silver medal of the Royal National Lifeboat Institution for his efforts, so it seems that everybody gained. Renamed *Lord Saltoun* after the Fraser landowner, the schooner would be commanded by 29 year old Captain John Noble and added to the sealing fleet. Noble was a Broadsea born man who had previously mastered *Active* of Peterhead, operating on the east coast of Scotland. His master's certificate was number 17532.

After the 1858 season, Fraserburgh had performed less creditably than on previous years. While the 29 Peterhead vessels gained nearly 71,000 seals and 31 whales with 947 tuns of seal oil, the five Fraserburgh vessels gained 11,649 seals, so their average for the year was less than Peterhead.

After the 1858 season, the Fraserburgh Seal and Whale Fishing Company showed a profit of £343 5/4d; this result was hardly a major success story and allowed no dividend to the shareholders. However, the directors of the company did say that the whaling ships were in good repair so no money need be spent on upgrading them. The company therefore looked upon 1859 with some optimism of making a fine profit. Indeed that year opened with the Fraserburgh sealing and whaling fleet at its largest, with six vessels preparing to take to the north. There had been hard times and hard weather, but the people of the Broch had taken their chances, exploited the situation as best they could and now hoped to reap the rewards of the northern oceans.

1859 season

By 1859 a wind of change was blowing through Scotland. On one side there was a new wave of temperance recruiting men and women in an attempt to stop the supposed threat of alcohol to the moral and physical health of the nation. Fraserburgh was not immune from this movement, and there were temperance meetings in the town. Added to that was a new wave of evangelical Christianity, powered partly by the Trans-Atlantic power of the revivalists Moody and Sankie and partly by the Great Disruption of the Church of Scotland in 1843, which saw the Free Kirk challenging the established, patronage ridden Church of Scotland for position. Fraserburgh had its own Total Abstinence Society, with the chairman none other than Mr Tindall Junior, the manufacturer of the harpoon gun.

Large numbers turned up for the Reverend Donald's pre-voyage sermon in the Free Kirk, with Greenlandmen among the congregation that packed the church and part of the vestry. The Reverend directed his sermon at the nautical section of his audience, while the collection was suitably dedicated to the Shipwrecked Fishermen and Mariner's Benevolent Society.

It was occasions such as this that revealed the duality of the Greenlandmen. On one side they had the reputation of being a hard swearing, hard drinking bunch, reckless in any situation and as liable to riot as to conform. However, in this instance at least they showed a devotion to a strict branch of Christianity that may not have been expected. The whaling men were perhaps a more complex bunch of people than was commonly supposed.

As always the Fraserburgh ships sailed in two groups, with the larger vessels leaving harbour around the middle of the month. *Melinka, Enterprise, Alexander Harvey* and *Vulcan* sailed for the sealing and whaling, with *Sovereign* and the new *Lord Saltoun* sailing a few days later. As in the previous season, *Melinka and Alexander Harvey* carried Mr Tindall's Fraserburgh made harpoon guns, hoping this year to use them to more effect. Once again the crowds watched them leave, and anxiety settled on the Broch when the women returned to their homes.

By April it seemed that the bottom had fallen out of the sealing industry with reports of damaged and lost ships. The Dundee screw steamer *Narwhal* returned from the ice with her bows stove in and paused at Peterhead to pass on her news. *Empress of India*, a brand new screw steamer had been sunk on the 20th March and her master, Captain Martin junior landed at Peterhead with tales of terrible weather in the north. He mentioned hard frost contracting the iron rivets so the ship leaked and the crew taking to the boats to be rescued by other vessels. Other vessels had also gone down: *Alert* of Peterhead had sunk, with her crew saved. *Kate* of Peterhead was damaged. *Volunteer* of Newcastle was lost, along with a black barque, whose name was unknown, while the screw steamer *Emmaline* of Hull had been forced home disabled. And worst of all for Fraserburgh was news of the loss of *Melinka*.

That news must have devastated the people of the Broch. *Melinka* had undoubtedly been the star in the Fraserburgh constellation, with consistently good catches. Now *Narwhal* reported that she had been lost on the 28th March, although all the crew, thankfully, were reported to have been saved.

It was interesting that of the total British sealing and whaling fleet of 54 vessels, 13 were screw steamers, but of the eight ships lost or forced to return damaged, five were also steamers. At that date there was speculation that screw steamers might be the future, while others believed they were not suitable for Arctic conditions. There were many people in Peterhead and probably in Fraserburgh too, who were not dismayed at the thought of steam ships going down, as sailing ships made up all the Fraserburgh fleet and the bulk of that of Peterhead. If screw steamers proved especially vulnerable to Arctic conditions, then the sail powered sealing ships would continue to thrive.

There was further bad news a few days later when the Fraserburgh vessel *Happy Return,* homeward bound from Dundee with a cargo of oil casks, was caught in a gale and capsized a few miles off Slains Castle. The master, David Elder, ushered the men onto the hull as she tipped over. A rescue boat from the shore, commanded by Willie Phillip and crewed by his sons, brought all the crew of *Happy Return* to safety, but nothing could be salvaged.

With the people of Fraserburgh depressed over the loss of *Melinka,* faint glimmers of good news now began to ease through the clouds. Ten days after the initial report of disaster, Captain Penny of the Hull whaler *Emma* brought back contradictory stories. Her master said that *Enterprise* had captured around 1,200 seals, but *Sovereign* was clean. More importantly, he believed that *Melinka* was not sunk, but was frozen in somewhere on the hunting ground. Captain Penny based his reasoning on evidence of the seals. He noticed that the seals on the outer streams of ice were unsettled and did not stay with the pups, which was a sure sign that they were being hunted. Captain Reid of the Peterhead sealer *Arctic* supported Penny, saying he supposed *Melinka,* as well as the reportedly sunk *Alert* to be frozen in.

While such speculation may have raised the hopes of the families of the missing Greenlandmen, it also reveals the agony of ignorance in which they lived when their men were absent. With no radio or other rapid communication, they survived on rumour and chance snippets of news. It is no wonder that so many fishing and maritime families were staunch worshipers at the church. Faith must have been a constant comfort when there was nothing else.

Toward the end of April another Hull vessel called at Fraserburgh carrying letters from *Lord Saltoun*. Captain Noble wrote that he had 55 tuns of oil, which would have pleased the shareholders, and also stated he had seen *Melinka* safe and well. The initial delight would have quickly faded when it was realised that Captain Noble's letter was dated 24th March, two days before the initial report that *Melinka* was lost.

The people of the Broch would remain anxiously watching the horizon, waiting news from anybody as they tried to continue with their day-to-day lives. By the 31st May *Lord Saltoun* had returned safely to Fraserburgh and there was more information about the whaling and sealing fleet. The screw steamer *Innuit* of Peterhead was sunk in the ice but all hands were safe. Some Hull and Dundee ships had returned unsuccessful, others had poor catches, *Perseverance* was trapped in the ice, *Polar Star* had 11,000 seals, and the Fraserburgh ship *Alexander Harvey* had been trapped in the ice since the 14th May, as had *Vulcan*, together with *Tay* of Dundee. Then came the good news, *Melinka* was beset, clean of whales but still afloat with her crew on board. It seemed that the fleet had been in good spirits and had high hopes of a good capture when the ice closed in suddenly and trapped them. Now all they had to do was sit tight and wait for a chance to break free.

There must have been joy among the families, mingled with concern at the coming winter, for with no seal oil to sell, the wages would be meagre and times hard. As the year wore on, the Fraserburgh vessels gradually came home. On the 20th June *Vulcan*, now commanded by another of the Stephen clan, Captain Peter Stephen arrived with 100 seals, and Captain Samuel's *Sovereign* arrived the same day with 75 seals. Captain Peter Stephen reported that both *Melinka* and *Alexander Harvey* were clean, but *Enterprise* had 35 tuns of oil. *Alexander Harvey* arrived in mid July, with the sad news of the death of one of her men. *Enterprise* arrived at the very beginning of August, and lastly, on the 23rd of the month, *Melinka* sailed in with a meagre cargo of four tons of oil but with every man present and accounted for.

The 1859 season then, had not been successful, but if the catches were poor, at least all the vessels had come home safely and only one man had died. Even so, the people of Fraserburgh must have looked to the 1860 season with more apprehension than normal.

Chapter Eight

THE FRASERBURGH SEAL AND WHALING INDUSTRY: THE 1860s

> We left the harbour of Fraserburgh on a cold and blustering day in February. The whole of the bonnie wee town was down to see us start and really there were more tears shed than there were handkerchiefs to dry
> Gordon Stables 1859

1860 Season
In the beginning of 1860, the Fraserburgh Greenland fleet was at its peak. The people of the Broch could look back on a roller-coaster ride during the previous decade, but they could also see that their fleet had gradually increased until it was one of the most sizeable in Britain, although a long way behind Peterhead. If they enlarged the harbour, and if catches improved on 1859, there was no reason why they should not increase their fleet further.

The season started well enough, with *Alex Harvey* and *Lord Saltoun* first away from harbour in the middle of February and Captain Sellar taking *Vulcan* out shortly after. *Dundee* of Dundee giving good reports of catches by the Fraserburgh vessels, and on the morning of the 18th May *Lord Saltoun* came in with a respectable 2000 seal skins and 27 tuns of oil. However, as she was being towed past the middle jetty into the inner harbour, her jib boom collided with a brick chimney. With the swell pushing forward the vessel, the twelve foot high chimney collapsed, causing casualties among the crowd that had gathered to watch her enter. Three people were hurt. A nineteen-year-old man named James Sim; servant to Mr Henderson of Aberlour had his skull fractured and for a while was in danger of his life. The twelve-year old James Grant, son of a local watchmaker had severe head and leg injuries, so one leg had to be amputated, and an elderly fisherman named William Stephen received more minor, but still painful, injuries.

The accident could have been worse but for the action of Captain James Day, who cleared people out of the way as the chimney fell. Ironically, the chimney was on top of an engine house being used to improve the harbour. It was not an auspicious start to the decade.

As usual, the ships returned one at a time, with *Alexander Harvey* back at the beginning of June, followed quickly by *Vulcan* with 600 sealskins and 11 tuns of oil. Not until October was there a report about the other vessels, with *Melinka* having caught two whales and carrying a cargo of 30 tuns of oil, while *Enterprise* often unlucky, was clean but still hunting.

Despite the relatively low catches, Fraserburgh's spirit remained high, with a regatta held on the third week of October. Lord Saltoun, with Sir John Bayley and Colonel Fraser all contributed to the total prize money of £22 for which the competitors rowed and sailed.

A tent was erected for Lord and Lady Saltoun at the New North Pier, and as soon as they sat down than four whale boats raced for Sir John Bayley's £5 prize. With each boat manned by six rowers, the representatives of *Sovereign*, *Lord Saltoun*, *Alexander Harvey* and *Vulcan* raced to a boat that was a mile out from the harbour, rounded it and returned. *Sovereign*'s crew came first, followed by *Lord Saltoun*, *Vulcan* and finally *Alexander Harvey*.

The high spirits and good feeling occasioned by the regatta, however, could not last. Within a month came news of the loss of *Enterprise* in Cumberland Gulf in the Davis Strait. On the 11th October she was at anchor but a squall hit her – the *Fraserburgh Herald* reported it as a 'hurricane' and drove her on to a reef. Mercifully, there were no casualties, and the crew set fire to the wreck. Although the *Herald* believed the fire was deliberately started to prevent the Inuit from robbing the wreck, it was common practise to first remove the spirits and then burn the wreck of a whaling ship. *Enterprise* was clean of oil or bone and the Peterhead whaler, *Sir Colin Campbell commanded* by the Ellon Born Captain Robert Birnie soon rescued Captain Burnett, and the crew. The company did not lose much money as *Enterprise* was insured for £4,000, but Fraserburgh's sealing and whaling fleet had been reduced to five.

The final Fraserburgh vessel, *Melinka*, only arrived back in Fraserburgh on the 28th November, with, for her, an unimpressive 35 tuns of oil. She had left a boat's crew behind in Davis Straits ready to try the whale fishing in the spring. The practise of overwintering among the Inuit of Eastern Canada was becoming very popular with the Scottish whaling crews, and seemed acceptable to the Inuit as well. The two peoples seemed to get along well enough, with cross-cultural exchanges and even some romance, so that Inuit children born and brought up among the ice may well have had a Scottish father. The lack of racism on both sides is an excellent example of how things could have been, and reveals the high toleration of outsiders among the indigenous peoples of the Arctic.

There are many examples of this relationship between Greenlandmen and the Inuit. As early as 1830 George Laing, surgeon on the Hull whaler *Zephyr* wrote: "We were visited by two of the natives in canoes...they came on board with all the familiarity imaginable." Some of the Scottish vessels brought Inuit people home with them, where they were charmed the Scots with their kayaking skills. The exchange of cultures was mutual, as in 1884 the Dundee vessel *Aurora* steamed up Lancaster Sound when an Inuit sang 'Bonnie Laddie, Highland Laddie' to them, while the Inuit of Pond Inlet enjoyed porridge, Scottish music and tea. If nothing else, the Greenlandmen proved that different peoples could mix amicably.

1861 Season

This season Fraserburgh sent out only three vessels. While *Sovereign* and *Vulcan* disappear from the sealing grounds forever *Melinka, Lord Saltoun* and *Alexander Harvey* sailed north on the 25th February, half the number of the previous year. *Lord Saltoun* was first to return on the 2nd April, and reported another difficult season with eight Peterhead vessels clean. *Lord Saltoun* had no sooner arrived than she was sent back north, sailing to Archangel under a Captain Brodie. That season was one of the most significant for the Scottish whale and sealing fleets, as well as for the long-term future of the Fraserburgh vessels.

The season was defined by the success and failure of two distinct sections of the whaling and sealing fleet. On one hand there was the failure of the old-style sail-powered vessels, on the other the final success of the steamers. There were two vessels lost, *Alert* of Peterhead and *Union* of Aberdeen, both sailing ships, but the steam powered screw whalers made large catches. For example the steamer *Narwhal* of Dundee caught 29 whales and brought back 200 tuns of oil, and the steamer *Tay* of Dundee caught 18 whales, with 123 tuns of oil. The sail powered *Chieftain* of Kirkcaldy caught 2 whales and brought home 30 tuns of oil.

By 1860, steam was not a novelty in Scottish shipping. The dream of steam power extended as far back as the 16th century, but the world's first commercial steam powered vessel had been the paddle steamer *Charlotte* Dundas. She was a small, open vessel, wooden built and with an engine by William Symington. Financed by Lord Dundas and named after his daughter Charlotte, in 1802 she chugged along the Forth and Clyde Canal, of which he was a governor, towing two lighters. The success of *Charlotte Dundas* prompted more Scottish engineering innovation and in 1812 *Comet,* Europe's first commercial sea going paddle steamer, sailed between the Broomielaw and Helensburgh. By 1820 *Comet* was operating off the Scottish west coast but ended her career that December in the disturbance known as the Dorus Mhor.

By that time, however, steam ships were relatively commonplace, and their rise began to challenge the sailing vessels that had dominated the seas for so many millennia. The New York built *Savannah* had crossed the Atlantic as early as 1819, but although she had an engine, she relied mainly on her sails. It was the Leith built *Sirius* that can justifiably claim to be the first vessel to cross the Atlantic under steam power alone, defeating the mighty *Great Western* by only a few hours.

Although paddle steamers were not thought suitable for the whaling and sealing trade, the development of the screw steamer gave rise to hopes that this new technology might be useful in the north. In the late 1850s, Hull, Peterhead and Dundee all experimented with screw steamers, and although the initial results were mixed, there were certain advantages. For example, steam powered vessels did not need to worry about favourable wind; they could manoeuvre with more ease and could ram their way through ice by using their engines. The downside was the initial cost of construction, the price of coal and the amount of cargo space that the coal used.

However, by 1858 steam screw vessels were operating in the Arctic. The Peterhead steamer *Innuit* worked in the ice with small success, and was sunk in 1859 but other steam ships were being built for the trade. In Dundee, the shipbuilders Gourlays installed a steam engine into a sailing ship and *Tay* chugged forth. She was 141 feet long, but her engine room accounted for 25 feet of that length, and her coal-bunkers consumed even more space.

Interestingly, although Dundee was to be the ultimate Scottish exponent of steam powered whaling ships, it was the Aberdonian William Penny who suggested such an innovation. Others, of course, also gave their opinions. For example there was a long and detailed letter in the *Banffshire Journal* of 04 November 1856. With the splendid title of 'On the Application of Steam Power to Vessels for the Whale Fishing,' the writer, John Anderson of the Royal Emporium in Edinburgh's George Street, gave his detailed advice to the whaling companies of Britain. After approving the fact that whaling companies were moving 'in a right direction' Anderson admits that paddle wheels would be inappropriate in the ice, but also says that neither would screws be suitable. Instead he suggests that whaling vessels should use Ruthven's Royal Propelling Motion that enabled 'a ship of any size' to be sailed by only a few men. Mentioning an instance when a Captain Claxton succeeded in freeing *Great Britain* from Dundrum Sands, by this method, Anderson wrote enthusiastically of a vessel that had successfully operated on the River Oder in Prussia for seven months.

Ruthven's method was to use steam power applied to powerful hoses that acted as jets, forcing the vessel through the water. According to Anderson, this method was easily controllable and had other uses on the ship. It is perhaps unfortunate that nobody followed up his suggestion of making 'a trial of this invaluable invention' for the idea of a steam powered jet ship in the Arctic is more than interesting. However, some whaling companies did push through with more conventional steam powered vessels.

The notable success of the steamers in the 1861 season revealed the way ahead. Progress had thrust its soot-stained thumb firmly on to the Arctic map and although sail powered craft would continue to battle northward for many more years, screw steamers dominate the closing decades of the Scottish Arctic whaling industry. There were many reasons for this alteration.

The whaling and sealing industry was operating in conditions that were steadily becoming more extreme as the whales withdrew further into the ice. With the necessity to venture into more dangerous waters for the whales, it was becoming apparent that sail powered ships lacked the necessary manoeuvrability and power. Steam ships could go astern and ram through thicker ice, while sail powered vessels could only rock themselves onward, or drop a ship's boat from the bowsprit onto the ice in front of them. In the season of 1861, the screw steamers often caught the whales in areas where the sailing vessels were in full view, but could not penetrate the ice.

Peterhead had been the leading Greenland port for some years, taking the place of Hull, and Fraserburgh had struggled heroically to build up a sealing and whaling industry to match. Now both were to be overtaken by a town that had greater resources and a steady market for whale and seal oil. Dundee had an established steamship building industry, Dundee had over a century of experience in whaling and Dundee required whale oil to soften jute for its expanding textile industry. Dundee would dominate British whaling in the final decades of the century, but if people in the Broch guessed that, they did not quietly lie down and surrender. They fought on with a losing hand but great determination.

1862 season

By now the Brochers may have realised that the best times of sealing and whaling were behind them. Left with only two vessels, they continued to hunt the sealing and whaling grounds, but they no longer thought about expansion. There was an old joke in Fraserburgh that when Peterhead sent out its large whaling fleet, the people of Fraserburgh retorted with humour. They used to display a notice at the pier. 'Half of our whaling fleet sailed yesterday,' the notice said, 'and the other half will leave tomorrow.' Presumably, that possibly apocryphal, story related to the closing few years of the Fraserburgh whaling industry, when only two ships sailed north.

The 1862 industry was quiet in Fraserburgh. The ships had to warp out of the harbour in the teeth of a brisk February wind, but both *Alexander Harvey* and *Melinka,* got out and both safely returned in what was to be a pattern for the next few years. The brig *Lord Saltoun* was now operating under new owners and sailed from Peterhead, although she was still registered at Fraserburgh. She returned to Peterhead at the beginning of June with only three tons of oil. As usual notices came in of the success of the vessels. On the 29th April it was announced that *Alexander Harvey* had 1600 seals, a figure that was increased to 2290 by the 13th May. She made a decent 33 tuns of oil that year; with *Melinka* bringing home 11 tuns more on the 11th of June. There were no dramas that year, just Greenlandmen doing their job under difficult conditions.

1863 season

1863 was much the same as the previous year, with the Fraserburgh ships sailing north under the command of the Stephen brothers at the end of February. The initial news was discouraging, with the screw steamer *Narwhal* of Dundee reporting that the seal fishing was poor but a later report saying the opposite, and claiming that while *Lord Saltoun* had arrived in Peterhead with 4,800 seals, she had sailed in company with *Melinka* and *Alexander Harvey*, who had been equally successful. Captain Murray of the Peterhead whaler *Queen* confirmed that by saying *Melinka* had 75 tuns of oil and *Alexander Harvey* 90 tuns, which would be a splendid result, particularly as the Dundee merchants were buying whale oil for £50 per tun that season. The high prices may be explained by Dundee's still expanding jute industry, which in turn was fuelled by the unsettled state of the world. With the American Civil War in full swing, armies needed sandbags, wagon covers and gun covers, all of which were made in Dundee, so more jute was needed, and therefore more oil to soften the brittle raw material. Fraserburgh was benefiting from the success of its rival whaling and sealing town. Both ships also carried well over 7000 high quality sealskins, which gave the trade a major boost.

1864 Season
Possibly because of the success of the previous season, Fraserburgh had renewed interest in whaling industry in 1864. The ship's crews signed articles, received their advance pay and, as usual, prepared to leave at the end of February. Again there was a pattern, with both the Church of Scotland and the Free Church preaching a sermon to the seamen before they departed. Reverent McLaren of the Church of Scotland preached from Acts 27: 14 'But soon a tempestuous wind, called the northeaster, struck down from the land.' Perhaps it had a nautical theme but such a sermon must have been a bit solemn before a dangerous voyage. The Reverent Smith of the Free Church chose Timothy 1:19 'holding faith and a good conscience. By rejecting conscience, certain persons have made shipwreck of their faith.' In other

words, he gave them a warning to live a good Christian life, in line with the evangelical atmosphere of the period.

In the event, the season was quiet. Both ships sailed on the 22nd February and returned at the end of June, with the Stephen brothers in command and neither shipwreck nor drama. *Melinka* captured around 2100 seals, and *Alexander Harvey* 1850, giving around 20 tons of oil apiece. Melinka had also rescued a boat's crew from *Emma* of Dundee that sunk on the 15th April. The pattern continued and Fraserburgh surely accepted that they had a small but steady sealing and whaling fleet.

1865 season
The year opened with a temperance meeting with a small and quiet audience, which may indicate that the impetus of temperance was fading. It was only a few days later that the two whaling ships were moved from their winter berths to be fitted out for the north. Bright weather brought large crowds to watch as the ships sailed on the 24th February and arrived back together in the middle of June. There had been high hopes for success that season, for the whaling men believed that there was a good crop of seals after a severe winter. They were not entirely wrong. *Melinka* brought back 85 tuns and *Alexander Harvey* 65 tuns of seal oil, so once again they made a solidly respectable voyage, but they also said that as the season lengthened the seals were becoming scarce.

No sooner had the sealing ships returned than there was news of *Lord Saltoun*. The schooner had been sold to Peterhead owners a few years before, but only that summer did the liquidators work out that the shareholders were entitled to £9 a share. This was a small reward, so they were not well pleased. Their investment in the sealing trade had not paid off.

1866 Season
This season started much the same as the previous years, with *Alexander Harvey* and *Melinka* preparing to sail around the middle of February. Once again there was a sermon for the Greenlandmen, but although the atmosphere in both the parish and the Free Church was

excellent, there were very few seamen present. The collection, again, went to the Shipwrecked Seaman's Fund, which was very appropriate as a gale arose the same weekend and the sealing vessels were unable to leave harbour until the 19th February.

Despite the enforced delay, however, the season started reasonably well, with both vessels watering at Lerwick and collecting between 30 and 40 tuns of oil by the 26th of April, and the ships heading north to hunt the old seals. Unfortunately, the old seals must have learned how to hide for six weeks of prowling around the ice proved fruitless and the ships arrived in Fraserburgh Bay in mid June with only thirty-four tuns of oil apiece.

Possibly because the season had been so poor, the Greenlandmen seemed to run wild when they received their less-than-generous wages that year. As well as the merry making, there was an injury, as two days before the wages were paid, Ian Noble, a hand from *Alexander Harvey*, fell into the hold and was badly bruised.

Fraserburgh's bad year continued in July when cholera came to the town, believed to have been brought in by a fisherman who had been to Stettin and France. By August the disease was raging, with three people dying on the 12th of August, three more on the 13th and one on the 14th. By the end of that month there were thirteen dead and the Highland fishermen, who came annually for the herring fishing, were beginning to leave for their homes. The cholera died away, to return in September, when the fishermen were prevented from going to sea and the town was subjected to rioting and drunkenness much more severe than anything created by the Greenlandmen.

1867 Season

1867 opened in the same old way, with the cholera burned out and the sealing companies determined to continue working in the north. The ships sailed together with Alexander Stephen commanding *Alexander Harvey* and John Stephen in *Melinka*. There was a slight alteration when an unidentified fever hit Shetland, so after sailing slightly earlier in February the two ships recruited extra hands at Stromness in Orkney instead.

After another uneventful season and a fast eight-day passage from the sealing grounds, both vessels arrived in Fraserburgh Bay in the middle of June. *Melinka* caught 3000 seals, making around fifty tuns of oil, but *Alexander Harvey* surpassed her with around seventy tuns. The state of the tide kept them in the bay for a few days, but their arrival was the sweeter for the delay.

Outside the seal hunting, 1867 was a busy time for the industry in Fraserburgh. The company directors sent *Alexander Harvey* to Newcastle to be refitted prior to the next season, with Captain Alexander Stephen accompanying her to supervise the work. After a few weeks in port, she sailed on the 17th July. Captain Stephen would sail with a touch of sadness as his brother, Captain Peter Stephen had died early in the month.

There were more developments that year as *Melinka* and all the other assets of the Fraserburgh Seal and Whale Fishing Company were auctioned off. The first attempt in August failed to find a buyer for *Melinka,* which was offered at £1000, but a second attempt at the Saltoun Hotel on the 21st October was more successful. James Cardno, a local fish curer and Justice of the Peace, was the leading light of the group that bought *Melinka* for £865, while other members of the public purchased the remainder of the company's assets. Cardno was no novice to the trade, having acted as the agent for both *Enterprise* and *Sovereign*. However there were some disturbing rumours in Fraserburgh that *Melinka* was only a successful ship because she had a lucky captain, and with Captain Stephen no longer in command, she would not be so fortunate in her catches.

After that, the Fraserburgh Seal and Whale Fishing Company was no more. Whaling and sealing, however, continued as James Cardno's company decided to repair and fit out *Melinka* for 1868.

1868 Season

At first this season seemed no different to most of its predecessors. There was the usual bustle at the beginning of February as the ships were prepared for the north, and the same two vessels sailing out. At first they were expected to sail before the 20th of February but both ships left two days later, on a fine morning with a huge crowd lining the quays and waving good bye. Although they could not have known it, they were witnessing the final departure of Fraserburgh's sealing fleet.

The new whaling company had replaced Captain John Stephen of *Melinka*, initially promoting Robert Duthie from his position as mate, but when the ships came to sail, a Captain Tait was in command. Alexander Stephen remained as master of *Alexander Harvey*. There was a change in the makeup of the crews, too. In previous years the ships had recruited about half their hands in the Northern Isles, but as the islanders preferred steamships, more local men sailed in 1868.

That was a poor year on the ice. Captain Tait's *Melinka* arrived back at Fraserburgh on the 10th May with 1100 seals, making 12 tuns of oil, and reported that *Alexander Harvey* had between 12 and 20 tuns. Captain Tait had returned back early from the north partly because *Melinka* was in poor condition and leaking and partly because he did not think there was much chance of increasing his catch. *Alexander Harvey* arrived at the beginning of June with 2,600 sealskins and 30 tuns of seal oil. Such a meagre catch was not enough to thrill the shareholders, for although it meant the company was in the black, there was no profit margin. That year had been a failure for Fraserburgh.

1869 season

Perhaps it was not surprising, given the previous poor season that in 1869 *Melinka* was transferred to Peterhead, where she operated under Captain Salmon, late of *Alert* of that port.

Alexander Stephen had left the sealing trade and took command of the newly built three masted schooner *Resolute*, bound for the Mediterranean and West Indies fruit trade. *Alexander Harvey* was also retired from the Arctic, although she remained in Northern waters in the Quebec timber trade.

After 1869 there was no formal Fraserburgh participation in the Arctic whaling or sealing trade. However, the Broch remained a very actively maritime place, with the herring industry going from strength to strength. Today Fraserburgh remains a vital fishing port, the largest white fish port in Europe and there are very few memories of the whaling that once caused so much excitement.

Chapter Nine

TAIL ENDERS

Sweet as the last song of a bird
Soft as a wind-swell from the Sea
Maurice Thompson

The demise of the Fraserburgh whaling industry marked the end of active participation in the trade by any of the Moray Firth ports. However, it did not mark the end of a Moray Firth connection. No doubt there would still be seamen from the firth serving on ships from other ports, and there were other vessels built along the Moray Firth that hunted in the Arctic.

In 1851 James Duncan, shipbuilders at Speymouth built a 330 ton vessel named *Spitzbergen* for a Peterhead whaling company. The Garmouth built *Ranger,* with its owners in Inverness and Garmouth, continued to sail from Aberdeen, and the Lossiemouth built *Chieftain* worked from Dundee, which soon replaced Peterhead as Britain's premier whaling port. *Chieftain* was a three masted carvel built schooner with a square stern and a male figurehead, weighing nearly 169 tons. Launched in 1868 and built by the Lossiemouth company of Jack, she sailed from Dundee until 1892, when the ice claimed her, as it did so many fine ships.

Only with the loss of *Chieftain* did the Moray Firth connection finally fade away. It had been a brief, but interesting period in a nautical coast, and is hardly remembered today. If the Scottish Arctic whaling industry is recalled at all, it is Peterhead or Dundee that is thought of, and it is unlikely if more than a handful of people from outside the ports of Banff and Fraserburgh know about the days that these ports sent their ships to the iced seas of the north. That is a pity, for, without arguing over the morals of whaling, there is no doubt that the men who ventured north were amongst the bravest and hardest working of any seamen, and the stories they told are worth recalling. Perhaps someday the Moray Firth will erect a monument to their memory, for even if Christian Watt did think them a 'wild rough lot' they were as much part of the history of the firth as the fishermen or traders.

Today Banff is a small town proud of its past and not quite sure of its future. It has a legacy of some splendid buildings that sit near the sea that created so much of its history, but where once whaling and trading ships sailed for profit and adventure, a marina hosts pleasure craft and great rollers batter Telford's Lighthouse pier. Few people are even aware that sealing ships sailed from the small harbour.

As a contrast, Fraserburgh has continued with its long maritime association. After the whaling came the herring, and the fishing industry plays a major part in the life of the burgh. Both loved by the sea: hopefully that connection will continue.

Appendix One

LIST OF WHALING SHIPS OF BANFF AND FRASERBURGH

BANFF

Vessel's Name	Seasons	Registered Tonnage	Master	Remarks
Earl of Fife	1814-1815		Wilson	Lost 1815
Triad	1813; 1815; 1818		Slater	
Felix	1852 – 1854	91 Tons	Fraser	Lost 1854
Alexander Harvey	1853-1855	292 tons	Hay	Sold to Fraserburgh

A Wild Rough Lot

FRASERBURGH

Vessel's Name	Seasons	Registered Tonnage	Master	Remarks
Alexander Harvey	1856 – 1868	292	Alexander Stephen, aged 31 in 1857; when Donald Hutcheson aged 54 was mate	Official number 10445 Registered at Peterhead. Manager was Charles McBeath
Melinka (barque)	1852 – 1868	297	John Stephen (aged 36 in 1857)	Manager was George Wallace, Her official number was 19553 and she was registered in Banff
Sovereign (brig)	1853 -1860	130	Burnett; Samuel	
Lord Saltoun	1858 - 1861	180	John Noble	
Vulcan	1852-1860	177	Alexander Noble (1856-57) Peter Stephen 1858	
Enterprise	1856 - 1860	397	Burnett	

Appendix Two

CREW LIST OF LORD SALTOUN 1859

Name	Age	Place of Birth	Previous Vessel	Capacity on Vessel
John Noble		Broadsea	Active, Peterhead	Master
George Noble	34	Fraserburgh	Louisa, Peterhead	Mate
William Cardno	32	Cairnbulg	Innuit, Peterhead	Harpooner
James Watt	36	Fraserburgh	Sovereign, Peterhead	Specktioneer
William Adam	21	Fraserburgh	Lady Saltoun, Peterhead	Harpooner
Alexander Noble	26	Fraserburgh	Ann, Banff	Harpooner
William Duthie	27	Inverallochy	First ship	Carpenter
James Adam	23	Fraserburgh	Nancy Riley, Newcastle	Boatsteerer/Bosun
Andrew Noble	45	Fraserburgh	Perseverance, Peterhead	Seaman
Andrew Adamson	25	Edinburgh	Eliza, Peterhead	Carpenter's mate; boatsteerer

A Wild Rough Lot

Name	Age	Place of Birth	Previous Vessel	Capacity on Vessel
John Buchan	49	Fraserburgh	Louisa, Peterhead	Cook
Donald Cameron	31	Inverness shire	Active, Peterhead	Line coiler
James Pirie	24	Rathen	Melinka, Banff	Line coiler
Donald McKenzie	35	Cromarty	Active, Peterhead	Line coiler
Stephen Buchan	21	Fraserburgh	Lady Saltoun, Peterhead	Boatsteerer
Robert Thomson	24	Rathen	Alexander Harvey, Peterhead	Line Manager
Alex McLeman	21	Fraserburgh	Alexander Harvey, Peterhead	Line Manager
Robert Fraser	44	Tain	Enterprise, Peterhead	Ordinary seaman
Alexander Pirie	23	Rathen	Kate, Peterhead	Line Manager
William Kidd	37	Forfarshire	Enterprise, Peterhead	Cooper
Archibald Campbell	28	Fraserburgh	Sovereign, Peterhead	Boatsteerer
John Noble	18	Fraserburgh	Providence, Carmarthen?	Ordinary seaman
James Miles	22	St Andrews	Roman, Peterhead	Line Manager
Robert Stephen	16	Fraserburgh	Isabella, Peterhead	Steward
Andrew McLeman	23	Fraserburgh	Perseverance, Peterhead	Ordinary seaman
George Noble	15	Broadsea	Andrews, Peterhead	Ordinary seaman
Alexander McLeman	17	Broadsea	First ship	Ordinary seaman
Forbes Massie	34	Fraserburgh	Agostina, Peterhead	Ordinary seaman
Robert Duthie	35	Cairnbulg	Vulcan, Peterhead	First Harpooner

Name	Age	Place of Birth	Previous Vessel	Capacity on Vessel
Robert Duthie	35	Cairnbulg	Vulcan, Peterhead	First Harpooner
Robert Duthie	29	Fraserburgh	Stephens, Inverness	Harpooner
William Tait	28	Cairnbulg	Pomona, Peterhead	Boat steerer and skeaman
John Buchan	27	St Combs	Vulcan, Peterhead	Boat steerer
William May	30	Cairnbulg	Vulcan, Peterhead	Line manager
John Summers	19	Cairnbulg	First ship	Ordinary seaman
Wilson Cardno	18	Cairnbulg	First ship	Ordinary seaman
James Sim	38	Pitsligo	Vulcan, Peterhead	Line Manager
George Mitchell	19	Pitsligo	Comet, Garmouth	Ordinary
William Sim	18	Pitsligo	Vulcan, Peterhead	Ordinary
Hugh Munro	19	Inverness	Strive, Sunderland	Line Manager
William Oliphant	29	Rathen	Resolution, Peterhead	Ordinary seaman
John Sim	22	Pitulie	Bayfield, Peterhead	Ordinary seaman
Angus Taylor	29	Tain	Sovereign, Peterhead	Cook's mate
Alexander Noble	24	Broadsea	James & Jessie, Peterhead	Boat steerer
Andrew Dunn	23	Glasgow	Louisa, Peterhead	Boat steerer
John Birnie	34	Pitsligo	Vulcan, Peterhead	Line manager
APPRENTICES				
Alexander Buchan		Fraserburgh		
William Melville	14	Fraserburgh		

William Duthie the carpenter did not sail; discharged 21 Feb 1859 due to bad health

Vessels are mentioned with their port of registry, rather than the port from where they sailed.

Select Bibliography

Aberdeen Journal
Archibald, Malcolm, *Whalehunters* (2004) Edinburgh
Archibald, Malcolm, Across *the Pond: Chapters from the Atlantic,* (2001) Latheronwheel
Banffshire Journal
Banffshire Journal; 'The North of Scotland Whale and Seal Fisheries'; 08 March 1853
Barque North Pole (from Leith to Davis Strait) by David Lyle, Master, 21 March 1837
Barron, William, *Old Whaling Days,* (1895) Hull
Campbell, Matthew, *of a Voyage to the Davis Straits aboard the Nova Zembla of Dundee 1884*
Clark, Captain G. W., *The Last of the Whaling Captains* (1986) Glasgow
Cranna, John, *Fraserburgh Past and Present* (1914) Aberdeen
Davidson, Captain Thomas, *A Journal of a Voyage from Dundee Towards the Davis Straits on board the Dorothy in 1834*
Dundee Archives Customs and Archives 70.11
Dundee Courier
Dundee University Archives MS 254/3/2/7; 254/3/2/8; 254/3/2/10
Dyson, John, *The Hot Arctic,* (1979) London
Flannery, Tim, (editor) the life and adventures of John Nicol, Mariner, (1822, 2000) Edinburgh
Fraser, David, *The Christian Watt Papers* (1983) Edinburgh

Fraserburgh Herald
Glasgow Herald
Hector Adams, account of his voyage in Victor, 1877
Hustwick, Ian, *Moray Firth: Ships and Trade*, (1994) Aberdeen 1994
Lubbock, Basil, *The Arctic Whalers* (1955) London
Journal of a voyage to Davis Straits aboard SS Narwhal 1874 by Thomas T Macklin, 29th August 1874
Kemp, Peter, (Editor), *The Oxford Companion to Ships and the Sea*, (1976) Oxford 1851 *Census of Banff*, Moray Heritage Centre, MF/B2/2-1
MacLeod, Innes (Editor) To the Greenland Fishing, (1979) Sandwich
Markham, Captain A. H. *A Whaling Cruise to Baffin's Bay and the Gulf of Boothia and an Account of the Rescue of the Crew of the Polaris* (1874) London
Moray Heritage Centre: Census of Banff 1851 M/F/B2/2-1
NAS; Privy Council Records: PC5/4, folios 40b & 41a; Edinburgh 1 February 1625: from the Council to His Majesty... to fish in Greenland.
New Statistical Account of Scotland: Banff, Edinburgh and London
Northern Ensign
Peterhead Sentinel
Rycroft, Nancy, Captain James Fairweather: Whaler and Shipmaster, his life and Career 1853-1933, (2005) Ripponden
Smith, Robert, Buchan, Land of Plenty (1996) Edinburgh
Stables, Gordon, 'The Story of the Arctic Ocean' in *The Weekly Scotsman* 03 October 1896
Starke, June, [transcriber] *Baffin Fair: Experiences of George Laing, a Scottish Surgeon in the Arctic Whaling Fleet 1830 and 1831*, (2003) Hull
Wanless, John, *Journal of a voyage to Baffin Bay aboard the ship Thomas commanded by Alex Cooke 1834*

Dear reader,

We hope you enjoyed reading *A Wild Rough Lot*. Please take a moment to leave a review in Amazon, even if it's a short one. Your opinion is important to us.

Discover more books by Malcolm Archibald at https://www.nextchapter.pub/authors/malcolm-archibald

Want to know when one of our books is free or discounted for Kindle? Join the newsletter at http://eepurl.com/bqqB3H

Best regards,
Malcolm Archibald and the Next Chapter Team

About the Author

Born and raised in Edinburgh, the sternly-romantic capital of Scotland, I grew up with a father and other male relatives imbued with the military, a Jacobite grandmother who collected books and ran her own business and a grandfather from the mystical, legend-crammed island of Arran. With such varied geographical and emotional influences, it was natural that I should write.

Edinburgh's Old Town is crammed with stories and legends, ghosts and murders. I spent a great deal of my childhood when I should have been at school walking the dark roads and exploring the hidden alleyways. In Arran I wandered the shrouded hills where druids, heroes, smugglers and the spirits of ancient warriors abound, mixed with great herds of deer and the rising call of eagles through the mist.

Work followed with many jobs that took me to an intimate knowledge of the Border hill farms as a postman to time in the financial sector, retail, travel and other occupations that are best forgotten. In between I met my wife; I saw her and was captivated immediately, asked her out and was smitten; engaged within five weeks we married the following year and that was the best decision of my life, bar none. Children followed and are now grown.

At 40 I re-entered education, dragging the family to Dundee, where we knew nobody and lacked even a place to stay, but we thrived in that gloriously accepting city. I had a few published books and a number of articles under my belt. Now I learned how to do things the proper way as the University of Dundee took me under their friendly wing for four of the best years I have ever experienced. I emerged with an honours degree in history, returned to the Post in the streets of Dundee, found a job as a historical researcher and then as a college lecturer, and I wrote. Always I wrote.

The words flowed from experience and from reading, from life and from the people I met; the intellectuals and the students, the quiet-eyed farmers with the outlaw names from the Border hills and the hard-handed fishermen from the iron-bound coast of Angus and Fife, the wary scheme-dwelling youths of the peripheries of Edinburgh and the tolerant, very human women of Dundee.

Cathy, my wife, followed me to university and carved herself a Master's degree; she obtained a position in Moray and we moved north, but only with one third of our offspring: the other two had grown up and moved on with their own lives. For a year or so I worked as the researcher in the Dundee Whaling History project while simultaneously studying for my history Masters and commuting home at weekends, which was fun. I wrote 'Sink of Atrocity' and 'The Darkest Walk' at the same time, which was interesting.

When that research job ended I began lecturing in Inverness College, with a host of youngsters and not-so-youngsters from all across the north of Scotland and much further afield. And I wrote; true historical crime, historical crime fiction and a dip into fantasy, with whaling history to keep the research skills alive. Our last child graduated with honours at St Andrews University and left home: I decided to try self-employment as a writer and joined the team at Creativia . . . the future lies ahead.

You might also like:

Like The Thistle Seed by Malcolm Archibald

To read first chapter for free, head to:
https://www.nextchapter.pub/books/like-the-thistle-seed-scots-abroad

Printed in Great Britain
by Amazon